THE SPACE CADETS' TREASURY OF FOOTBALL NOSTALGIA

2097

JEZ PRINS
AND
DEREK HAMMOND

WITH ILLUSTRATIONS BY
SIMON SMITH

MAINSTREAM
PUBLISHING

EDINBURGH AND LONDON

Copyright © Derek Hammond and Jez Prins, 1996
All rights reserved
The moral right of the authors has been asserted

First published in 1996 by
MAINSTREAM PUBLISHING COMPANY (EDINBURGH) LTD
7 Albany Street
Edinburgh EH1 3UG

ISBN 1 85158 854 X

A CIP catalogue record for this book is available from the British
Library

Designed by Janene Reid
Colour reproduction by Zig Zag Communications, Glasgow
Printed and bound in Great Britain by Butler & Tanner Ltd, Frome

Yo!?! Switched-on football cat!?!

Welcome to my treasury of fan-tastic football fun!?! It is the sort of treasury that people will see you reading and automatically think you are cool and trendy!?!

Exactly *how* cool and trendy???

If **OASIS** were still alive today, they would really dig having millions of fascinating futuristic football facts at their fingertips!?! Even **FRANK WORTHINGTON** could learn groovy new ball-balancing tricks from my space-based skill-tips!?! **JULIA ROBERTS** would probably be really interested in my hobby ideas!?! **LADY DI**'s cryogenically frozen head says football in space is rubbish.

Mega cool and trendy!?!

People will probably start mistaking you for **BRYAN GIGGS** if you spend all your pocket-credits on stuff from my Merchandising Dept.

SAMMY SPACE CADET

This Book Belongs To

. . . .

OFFICIAL SPACE CADET

Worth a Goal's Start

Earth-players travel so widely there could be any number of reasons why the home support they encounter is worth the proverbial one-goal start. We commissioned a planet-wide pros' poll to find which away fans are the scariest, weirdest or hardest to fathom. These are the official five to fear.

5TH PLACE — TRAGAAV EAST

Reason Nominated: Because of the vicious storms that continually batter the planet, Tragaavians have incredibly well-developed, larnyx-like organs to make themselves heard over the howling gales. But because the state-of-the-art Tragaadome is insulated against external noise and holds 100,000 home fans, visiting teams are obliged to wear ear-muffs of elaborate design and industrial strength and, even on 'quiet' days when nothing more than animated chatter fills the ground, it's impossible to communicate with teammates. Since last year's gruesome and cowardly synchronised ear-drum explosions, a codicil to the Pan-Galactic FA's Rules & Regulations asserts that Tragaav East shall 'immediately forfeit any home match in the course of which more than ten home fans are independently judged simultaneously to boo, sneeze or sing.'

SONIC BOOM . . . Janet Seaman prepares for the Tragaavdome

Sample Poll Comment: 'It's not the noise so much as having to wear them poncey ear-muffs. You know the Tragaav lads are taking the piss, but you can never sort it cos you can't actually hear them.'

4TH PLACE — LABRAMINAX

Reason Nominated: On Earth we imagine we have a pretty broad-minded, inclusive idea of what constitutes 'music'. Different societies, traditions, cultures all have different ideas about rhythm, harmony, etc. But even our most seasoned and widely travelled musicologists have been reduced to fever and delirium on exposure to what passes for music on Labraminax. And those Labraminax fans do like a bit of a sing-song. Unlike Tragaav East, volume's not the problem, more the unique combinations of sounds produced by the 20–30,000 crowds. 'It's the frequencies,' says expert Dr Rolf Mankewicz, 'just as a diva can shatter glass with the right note, so a chorus of Labraminacs can find the right frequency to cause human organs actually to oscillate. It can be uniquely uncomfortable.'

Sample Poll Comment: 'We were three down, so they were gloating. It must have been their version of "You're shit, and you know you are" or something. But it felt like someone had let loose a bag of live frogs in me guts. I couldn't handle it. It's in me contract now, I'm never going back.'

3RD PLACE
PELLETATH

Reason Nominated: On Pelletath, players and fans are all telepathic mutes. Perhaps not as overtly hostile as a really noisy ground, Pelletath gets players' votes because of the highly sinister atmosphere evoked by thousands of fans making absolutely no noise. And, because they're all telepathic too, silence doesn't bother the home players a bit, so they can be hugely lifted by the right thoughts all being simultaneously thought. And the power of collective thought transmission has convinced many non-telepathic visitors that the crowd is, in effect, screaming high-decibel abuse at them.

Sample Poll Comment: 'Scariest place I've ever been, no question. I'd sooner have 60,000 screaming I'm a wanker than have half that give me a really nasty look and say nothing at all.'

PELLETATH . . . 'A really nasty look'

A SING-SONG . . . on Labraminax

2ND PLACE
MUSKA-MUSKA

Reason Nominated: As simple as it's horrible. Muska-Muskans are intelligent, sophisticated and hospitable, but, to the human ear, their voices sound just like a domestic housefly. It might be a bit of background buzzing, or a concerted attempt at a chant, but it still sounds like a swarm of big fat bluebottles bouncing round a very small room.

Sample Poll Comment: 'Disgusting. I don't mean no disrespect, some of them are nice enough lads. But the crowd, I mean, you're one on one with their keeper and the sound they make, it's like, instinctively, you start flapping your hands about cos you could swear there's a load of flies round your head.'

1ST PLACE
DUZROVIL

Reason Nominated: There is no sadder place to play. Duzroviles have so ruined and toxified their atmosphere that they're forced to live underground in a controlled environment. Their team's full of players from other planets, who – unlike the locals – are not acutely allergic to the atmosphere. Matches are played on a surface a little like Earth's old astroturf, only transparent. The crowd stands beneath the pitch, watching the game unfold above. A sensitive race, Duzroviles share a huge collective guilt about the havoc they're wreaked, and their body language – shrugs, sighs and a shuffling gait – reflects this. Rather than rush to the touchline, home players throw themselves face down on the transparent pitch to celebrate goals with their fans. The fans smile up at them, weakly. Away fans are made welcome; Duzroviles like to see them enjoy themselves in the stands they used to occupy – it reminds them of what their stupidity has forced them to miss. Duzroviles are the only race able to recognise players purely by the soles of their boots and the swell of their buttocks.

Sample Poll Comment: 'Some lads fake injuries to avoid this one. It's too sad, it's like playing at someone's funeral. Not easy to get pumped up for it. Plus you know a few of them are just looking at your arse.'

SKILL IN SPACE

Take a trip to Planet Tip-top Tip. And remember, in space, no one can hear the offside whistle . . .

SHILTON'S TRANSPORTER TRAP

Rygel 4's veteran understudy Peter Shilton is still playing at 147. Which would be major sporting news if he were playing snooker, but of course Shilton is a footballer. Or a goalie, at least – one of those scruffy, twitchy types who hang around with footballers. Shilton made his League debut at the age of 16 in 1966, which means he has been an ever-present across three-quarters of professional football history. It also means the great perfectionist has had to start cheating.

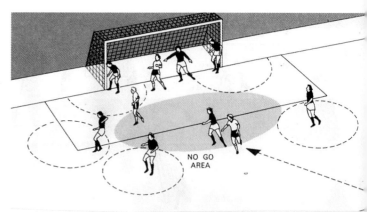

This X-ray photo of the Rygel Rangers penalty-box exposes how Shilton has concealed a vast Star Trek-style transporter pad under the playing surface, so he can whisk your team's forwards back to the dressing-room just when they're clean through on goal.

But hold on. Grandpa Shilton says he can't recall burying any new-fangled electrical devices on any pitch. He reckons those circles are just natural mushroom rings growing in the grass. And he says he's willing to put his money where his goalmouth is . . .

KLINGON INVASION ALERT!

Klingon tactics differ slightly from those employed elsewhere in the known universe, as the Mighty And Fearsome Home Planet XI have no conception of defence.

The typical Klingon 1-1-8 attack formation (Fig. 1) lends itself to a bloody battle to the death in the opposition penalty-box. Unusually, the back player is not a defender in the Klingon scheme – his sole role is to deal the goalkeeper a merciful and honorable warrior's execution if a goal is conceded. Or even if he drops a swirling cross. No messing.

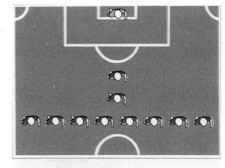

Formation G–1–1–8

Fig. 2 shows the ultra-defensive 2-2-6 formation adopted during Don Howe's short reign as Klingon coach, before his tragic demise at half-time.

The Klingon XI would like to announce they are currently seeking friendly fixtures on their 2098–99 pre-season tour/invasion of Federation space.

SHAPESHIFTING SHENANIGANS

Vital advice for terrestrial teams drawn against other-worldly outfits capable of shapeshifting, or controlled physical transformation:

1. Do not bother to attempt to score. That set of goalposts is probably a shapeshifter's ruse to get you to pass him the ball.
2. Do not bother to attempt to tackle a shapeshifter. The ball you see is in fact the shapeshifter's team-mate. The ball is in the back of your team's net.
3. Do not play to the referee's whistle. The referee's whistle may be a shapeshifter.
4. Do not give up the game and retire to the pub for a consolatory sherbet. That pint of alcoholic refreshment may be a shapeshifter.
5. Save rocket fuel – withdraw with grace from this season's F.U. Cup and hope you draw the Clangers next year.

Here we see experienced Arsenal centre-half Frank McLintock being taken on and left for dead by Arthur Lomax of Planet Claire. A shapeshifting version of the body-swerve was employed to get the better of the solid Caledonian stopper: Running straight at the stalwart defender, Lomax turned himself into a chicken biriani, dived expertly into McLintock's mouth, passed at lightning speed through his digestive system, emerged triumphant and sped on his way goalward.

NOBBY STILES

I wasn't unhappy. I'd been lucky. I'd played for Man United, won a few things, played for England, won the World Cup, but it had got so that all I was known for was tackling, false teeth and skipping. And it's all very well being a – what d'you call it? – a talisman, but I wasn't satisfied, and I don't think it's selfish to want more.

Funny, though. On Vigudon, they say they can read Earthlings' minds. They say we're weak, transparent and so on. Well, I don't know about that, but they certainly knew all about me when they came looking. I'd just finished me Frosties. House was empty so I was having a sly fag with the patio doors open, reading the paper, when suddenly there's this almighty white light at the bottom of the garden. Well, I knew it wasn't the sun shining off the greenhouse; for one thing the light was that bright I couldn't look, and for another, the sun doesn't get round to the greenhouse till gone teatime. I had some carp – pricey ones, mind – in a pond down there, and I thought they might be distressed, but there was no time to fret.

This big lanky fella comes up the path. (I say 'fella', but you could tell he wasn't right, not human as such. He had this shiny, bluish look, not a stitch on, and if you'd carved him to the bone you'd not have found the meat for a Danish sandwich.) He had a way about him, though. I'll say that.

Couldn't for the life of me place his accent, but he says: 'Nobby, come. There's a life on Vigudon to live in your name.' Well, I couldn't make head nor tail of him, so I says: 'Never mind that, state your business or be on your way. And get your big ugly feet off me delphiniums.' So he starts again, slower. Turns out he's head-hunting. Wants me to help launch the game on Vigudon. Apparently, being short's a help. They're all big long streaks over there, high centres of gravity, always falling over. So compact's a bonus. Plus, the attraction is – and bear with me because it's a head-stretcher – I don't actually have to move, just agree. That way, I get to stop here, in effect, while they sort of transmigrate me double, build another Nobby, so to speak, and he gets weaving with the coaching and such.

I don't lack a challenge now. I've got me life here – family, friends, garden, fish – only now, when I'm 'asleep' I'm not really 'asleep' at all, I'm away on Vigudon. The missus has got me under the doctor, mind, and he's put me on tablets for what he calls me 'nocturnal delirium and hallucinatory bouts', whatever that is when it's at home! Tell you what though, that day the light shone over me pond: best day I've had since '66. Lucky day for Vigudon as well, if I do say so myself!

UEF GOT TO BE JOKING!

The year 1998 saw European football's biggest ever shake-up, and here's the memo that did the shaking! Revolutionary then, the format was duplicated throughout the century to become a template for world, galactic and universal tournaments. Space Cadets can now enjoy the historic original, helped by this easy-to-follow illustration by THE TREASURY's top diagrammatic artist.

CHAMPIONS CUP

32 champions, seeded and drawn into eight groups of four. Due weight granted to clubs from leading nations as determined by agreed grading criteria, i.e. i) performance of National XIs at under-19 and under-21 level, ii) sponsorship-per-chairman indices, iii) average peaktime 30-second advertising spend, iv) executive box per hectare of available retail floorspace and v) proximity to Brussels. Subsidiary groups drawn from nations with military-run airports and/or Islamic régimes and/or vegetable-based economies to play off to qualify for special two-team group with Manchester United (the 'Automatic Bye').

UEFA CUP

Initially limited to 144 teams, comprising top six in all nations with due weight according to above mentioned criteria, also including first-round knockouts from preliminaries of Champions Cup ('Rangers'). Additional weighting granted to clubs from country with best disciplinary record, from country with highest per capita GDP and to clubs sponsored by Japanese electrical giants. Home and away ties decided on away goals, extra time, penalties, knock-out whist, one-potato, two-potato and/or dip dip dip, my blue ship.

CUP-WINNERS' CUP

For cup-winners, their friends, and, for most-favoured nations, clubs managed by ex-internationals.

THE INTER-IBIZA CUP

Formerly the Inter-Toto, renamed and repackaged to appeal to reluctant nations. Any club not actually relegated eligible (flexible stipulation, Waiver Form 2/9c.8 available from UEFA rep). Games played over two legs in Ibiza, Benidorm, Magaluf, Tenerife, Rhodes and/or Albufeira: two-hour half-times, shirts v skins, no away goals or deciders as above, but a Karaoke Challenge and/or Cocktail Race.

MILLENNIUM SHIELD

For teams relegated from top two divisions in all nations. Tournament to embody themes of Hope and Regeneration, chiming with advent of millennium. Games on Mondays, kick-off 10 a.m. sharp.

MILLENNIUM PLATE

For teams knocked out in first round of above. Note: Plate to be ceramic, blue willow pattern.

EURO-FEEDER VASE NORTH & EURO-FEEDER VASE SOUTH

For any club still without a game. Entrants from above/below line from Bordeaux to Stavropol (45 degrees north, teams on line itself need Polar Determination Form 62/1.6a from UEFA rep).

THE GARY BOWL

For teams fielding at least three players called Gary. Should at least guarantee Leeds a European run. Birth certificates to be vetted by UEFA for deed poll irregularities.

Space Cadets: sign up now for a fan-tastic football nostalgia language course. Simply touch the authentic original star message you would like to deliver. Listen to the futuristic miniaturised computer recording, and repeat. Drop casually into conversation – wow chums and chumettes with your amazing antiquated soccer slang.

Speak like the Stars

No.1:
Blathah like a Geordie, Thelma, pet . . .

Blubber and Gurgle with Paul 'Ga-Ga' Gascoigne

Rangers and England star Paul Gascoigne was a giant baby. The highest mental age he ever attained was allegedly 3¹/4. Call your partner's attention to the imminent arrival of feeding-time with the following authentic Geordie-style tempah-tantrum:
'Ga-ga goo-goo [*raspberry noise*] goo-goo ma-ma boo-boo [*burst into tears*] ga-ga ma-ma boo-boo wor Sheryl lass.'

Appreciating Nature with Wor Jackie Charlton

Phrase one: 'Howay, ye see yon canny hurd o' reindeeyahs urvah thayah, like? See the blurk reindeeyah's geet magnificent antlahs? See the tottie reindeeyah's big sausah eyes an' shite – an' that frisky bairn reindeeyah sur reminiscent of wor Bambi Gascoigne?'
Old adage: 'Yow cannat make a luggage set withoot blastin' a few heeds.'

Giving it 110% with Manager Marvel

Bryan Robson was not technically a Geordie, but people of proper 'mainland' Britain never could be bothered with all those stupid petty north-east sub-groups anyway.
Phrase one: 'Haddaway an' shite, ye cahlin' me a Geordie pufdah? Ah'm a Teessidah Mackem Weahsidah an' prood, me, like.'

Win friends and influence team-mates! Speak Like the Stars and bring famous England manager Robson's tactical flair to bear at your next kickaround!
Phrase two: 'Howay an' give it 110%! Stop shur-in' off, man lad. Mebbe's yow do playah fowah Brazil an' shite but ye should ha' went for gurls more direct though but. Bollocks to yer crood-pleasin' hurmursexual foreplay skills an' bahl-contrurl, Mistah sur-curled Juninhur.'

LOVELY ACTION ... NOW LET'S TRY IT WITH A BALL!

Alternative Marvel vocab:

'Dislurcate yow shouldah' = Giving it 110%
'Breakin' thrur tha pain barriah' = Giving it 110%
'Youse lot lurn ta gan in urvah tha bahl' = Giving it 110%
'Youse lot take nehr prisonahs or yeer deed' = Giving it 110%

31 BRIAN LITTLE

Economy with the Truth and Brian Little

Phrase 1,976 (cont'd from page 121): 'Ah divvent knur why they curl me tha Little Lyah at owah football club though but. Ah happen thur jealous cos Ah'm marryin' Jur-annah Lumleh an' thur not like. She got 30 goals fo' owah football club last year, ye knur. People at owah football club say she urnleh fancies me cos o' me New Avangeahs look, like, but Ah sweer on tha Hurly Bible Ah've nevvah had a burl haircut in ma hurl life man lad,' etc. etc.

They called it . . .
'MACHO'

Vulcan soccer-ologist DR. SKORN on the objective historical truths of ten pints of fizzy lager and a chicken biriani . . .

Fighting. Swearing. Shouting. 'Mooning'. All cornerstones of the primitive football-related behaviour pattern we classify as 'macho'.

Until recently, this mind-set has been considered abhorrent, an incidental by-product of sports-based bonding rituals, group drug-abuse and/or the typical Space Age IQ of just 100.

But now I present controversial new evidence that suggests modern footballers' performance may be positively enhanced by clinically-controlled 'macho sessions'. Also, I compute that even today's advanced spectators may derive additional amusement from the game when administered with dosages of ancient herbal poisons...

CIGARETTES AND ALCOHOL 1: CIGARETTES

Cigarettes were rolled-up tubes of dried tobacco plant. When ignited and inhaled, nicotinic acid caused the 'smoker' to feel slightly nauseous in the short-run, and to expire in the longer-term. Cigarettes were universally discredited in the 1970s.

But back in the 1960s, nicotine clearly assisted this player - an enthusiastic addict - to win the FA Cup. A conspiracy of 'bad press' in the late 1960s period must logically be suspected.

Footballers of today: You too can be glamorous, sophisticated and a master of ball skills. Note: a 'Now' nicotine addiction may be initialised by employing stick-on patches, which feed the drug direct into the bloodstream. Old stocks of these devices, previously thought quite useless, are still available from most chemists.

CADETS
The **NOW** cigarette for the **NOW** people

COLE'S ANGELS

Andy Cole once played football at the very highest level for Newcastle, Manchester United, Manchester United Reserves, Scunthorpe, and Kidderminster Harriers. In very nearly consecutive seasons.

Andy Cole was 'trouble' - a leather-clad, gun-crazy Hell's Angel on a mission from Lucifer. This ultimate 'macho-man' would regularly bite the head off a chicken, park his 'hog' in Kevin Keegan's reserved parking-space, and flaunt team training at a Newcastle city-centre discotheque. Imagine the disappointment of Manchester manager Alex Ferguson when he discovered he had traded the club silver for a striker who urinated on his own coat.

PETER SHILTON'S AMAZING MACHO MUSCLE POWER

In many respects, Rygel 4's veteran understudy goalkeeper Peter Shilton is the living embodiment of Macho. He gambles.

He still takes his shirt off at every possible op-

'BULLWORKER gives me that *extra* muscle power' says PETER SHILTON

portunity. Usually because he's just lost it on a rocket race. His perfect pectorals are beautifully preserved in alcohol. And, oh yes. He's easily the greatest shotstopper in football history.

'I'll give you 5-to-1 I can still squeeze this Bullworker thing and score 100,' he says, taking his shirt off in preparation.

Shilton flexes and takes the strain . . . 'Phew! Er, best of three, all right?'

CIGARETTES AND ALCOHOL 2: ALCOHOL

In preparation for a football match of 150 years ago, it was customary for supporters to first drink ten pints of warm, lumpy-brown 'beer', a popular depressant made by decaying oats in water. Victory would be celebrated by players and fans alike - with ten pints of 'beer'. If a defeat was suffered, commiserations would be shared under the influence of ten pints of 'beer'.

When the era of this so-called 'Gary Glitter' beverage gave way to a fizzy, yellow form, many fine players prospered on a refreshments-only diet. Supporters were known to chat pleasantly with rival fans on the British Rail network, to demolish unsightly motorway service-stations, display their naked bottoms from speeding car windows and impinge on the rights of fellow life-forms such as females and curry-house waiters. In the strictest utilitarian economic terms, this 'macho' behaviour must now be applauded, maximising as it does the individual's available pleasure.

MACHO GESTURING FOR BEGINNERS

'Flicking the Vs': Form first and second fingers into 'V' shape, and direct at target. An aggressive manual gesture which has its roots firmly in the pre-verbal cro-magnon stage of man's development, when The Wanderers and Blackburn Rovers were capable of winning the FA Cup.

'Dickhead': Form circle with first and second fingers and motion away from forehead. A severe insult which likened the target to one-time West Ham full-back Julian Dicks.

'Wankaaaaah': Here demonstrated forcefully by a Leicester team that includes three of football history's great 'softies' - Alan Smith, Mark Bright and Big Bob Hazell - previously held up as paragons of politeness. Gary Winston Cojones Lineker is caught in characteristic mood.

A SUITABLE CASE FOR TREATMENT?

The great Paul Gascoigne is a magnificent advert for the revival of Macho. His football talent was expertly complemented throughout his career by an astonishing armoury of textbook adolescent attention-seeking. And demands that the media leave him well alone.

On the field of play, opposition players were bemused by Gazza's tactic of wearing plastic comedy breasts, by his suicidal tackling lunges, by his celebratory miming of an Orangemen's march, by his white hair / red hair / extended hair / no hair / purple 'mohican' cut, tears of joy, tears of laughter . . .

In his private life he kept up his magnificent record of Inappropriate Social Behaviour, obsessively burping into microphones, compulsively attempting to give losing contestants on 'Noel's Full House' a pocketful of money 'for the bairns' and, perhaps least impressively, admitting to being unable to leave the house until he was quite certain his towel was hung squarely on the radiator.

TAKE THE TEST-OSTERONE

At the height of the 'Macho Era', this practical etiquette test appeared in match-day magazines across the Midlands. Sponsored by a manufacturer of alcohol, it was designed to ensure a uniformity of behaviour on match-day. It also served to prevent embarrassing lapses into unacceptable topics of conversation in the 'public house', a rudimentary leisure-centre where humans gathered to buy each other drugs and argue over televised football on Monday nights.

The test now serves as an informative reprogramming guide for modern-day players and fans who may wish to access the manifold advantages associated with membership of the sub-group Homo Erectus Georgibestus. Initially, disregard all logic and foster an interest in the following Macho concerns:

1 - **FOOTBALL TRIVIA** Learn by rote each of the 139 teams who have won the FA Cup since 1958.
2 - **TRANSPORT** Engage in conversation with your space scooter.
3 - **BIRDS** Take up ornithology, specialising in European species and their habitats.
4 - **WOMEN** Attempt to discover the true birthline of your partner.
5 - **ALGEBRA** If someone calls you an A, B or C, make the correct response, '$A^2 + D = 54$'.

THE GREATEST-EVER ALL-TIME
SCOTLAND XI!

1. GLASGORANGEA
2. WALLACE
3. SCOTT
4. MONSTER
5. FAMOUSFIVE
6. MARINELLO
7. DALGLISH
8. GASCOIGNE
9. JORDANGRAY
10. HAMISH
11. BRAZIL

1. Gladioli GLASGORANGEA

Early this century, genetic engineers struggled long and hard to solve the eternal Scottish goalie problem. In 2025, botanists finally developed a successful shotstopping plant strain, which within months had made its Euroleague debut - for Partick Thistle. Gladioli Glasgorangea was designed with petals which closed around the goal-bound ball, alerted by sensitive hairs which detected the movement of objects in the air. The big plant lad was dug up at half-time, wheelbarrowed down to the other end and re-potted in time for the second-half. The succulent sticksman pulled on the hallowed padded scribbly jersey of his country 96 times before picking up a lifetime WFA ban for mistakenly ingesting the bald pate of his international boss Alan Hansen.

2. William WALLACE

Billy Wallace was one of the first great Scottish defenders. His taste in blue make-up was revived by Bet Lynch and Scottish away fans some ten centuries after his death, but his Darren Peacock hairdon't was a style only ever taken up by Darren Peacock. In the movie of his career, Billy was played by Mad Max.

3. Mister SCOTT

Scottie out of Star Trek shines like a dilithium crystal on the left of the new FU Cup champions' defence. A powerful intergalactic overlapper, Mister Scott is noted for his, ahem, good engine.

4. Loch Ness MONSTER

Up until as late as 2010, our backward ancestors questioned the very existence of the Venusian families who made the long caravan trip to holiday in the central highlands. Altogether more predictable was the human furore when one muckle beastie's ball-skills were recognised by a Rangers talent-scout. Did Venusian fish-worship count as a distant branch of catholicism, or what?

5. FAMOUSFIVE

Turnbull Ormond Reilly Smith Timmy the Dog FamousFive was a goalscoring legend for Hibs in the 1950s. He was so extravagantly gifted that when he made his international breakthrough, no-one even thought to note down the names of his four striking partners.

BODYSNATCHER INVASION ALERT! BODYSNAT INVASION ALERT! BODYSNATCHER INVASION

6. Peter MARINELLO

When Arsenal paid Hibs £100,000 for Marinello in 1970, the London media keenly claimed the dainty flanker as the New George Best - which meant he got to share hair-ironing tips in 'Jackie' and boogie about on Top of the Pops. This stop-action photo-sequence of his metamorphosis explains Little Lord Fauntleroy's sudden disappearance – and the spooky overnight emergence of Leeds' Allan Clarke.

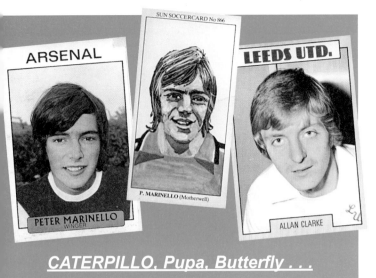

ARSENAL — PETER MARINELLO WINGER

SUN SOCCERCARD No 866 — P. MARINELLO (Motherwell)

LEEDS UTD. — ALLAN CLARKE

CATERPILLO, Pupa, Butterfly . . .

9. Connery JORDANGRAY

A recent android signing for Glasgow United, Jordangray is programmed with the authentic attributes of all the classic Scottish centre-forwards. He dives fearlessly to stick his head between boot and ball. His front teeth are fully detachable. He has 'Scotland Forever' tattooed on his forearm. He's tasty with his fists, his nut, his pro-celebrity mashie-niblick and his service-issue Walther PPK. And female hearts melt when he says 'Poosy'.

10. Hot-Shot HAMISH

Prolific fat Highland Leaguer Hamish's apparently nonsensical battle-cry of 'Ah'll smack yon bladder in yon lobster-pot the noo, y'ken' was recently translated from the Ancient Caledonian as, 'Come 'n' ha' a gae, ye wee spamheed referee bastad, aaaanyway.'

7. Kenny DALGLISH

King Kenny of Celtic and Liverpool was the first name on the teamsheet. But only to prevent him going for the manager's job: one All-Time Greatest team left in ruins is more than enough for one career.

8. Paul GASCOIGNE

Having been resident in Glasgow for four years, Gazza made a successful post-Bosman claim for home-player status - and an automatic spot in the Scottish midfield - in 1999. Few knowledgeable Scots fans would now argue the selection of a barking Englishman in their All-Time XI ahead of fluffy comedian Denis Law.

11. Alan BRAZIL

Brazil brought his silky South American skills to the Scotland team late last century, coincidentally at the same time Jordan was contributing his trademark Arabian spice. Correspondingly during this era, Mike England appeared for Wales. Simon Garner (Blackburn, West Brom, Wycombe) regularly

ALAN BRAZIL — IPSWICH TOWN

turned out for the Netherlands. And, logically enough, West Ham's Patsy Holland pulled on the hallowed green, orange and turquoise nylon of Ghana . . .

FIRST-ROUND HIGHLIGHTS

FOOTBALL UNIVERSE CUP 2097

LAND OF THE GIANTS 3
X-FILES 1

Agent Fox Mulder isn't just the spitting image of Chelsea's Dan Petrescu, he plays full-back like him too. With Fox too busy hunting for openings in the oppo box, the 70-foot L.O.G. lads humped the ball big into the FBI corners, and hit paydirt.

Long after the match - even after she'd been un-sellotaped from the giants' desktop - Agent Scully was still stubbornly skeptical about the probability of a team from another footballing dimension going route one . . .

LADY P and TB chairman Alan Sugarsmack

Other results
SPACE 1999, APOLLO 13
NEXUS 4, BLAKE'S 7
BLUR 0, OASIS 1

ALIEN 0
THUNDERBIRDS 5

The big dinosaur soccerette had no answer to the formulaic game-plan of International Rescue. With most of her team still in the egg stage, Alien was stretched thin at the back, and the marionettes ran rampage with Brains and Mr. Tracy pulling strings in midfield. Although rarely called upon, Thunderbirds goalie (well, he was playing in TB 1) Scott made at least one heroic save per episode.

Controversy surrounded some ungentlemanly tactics from the Alien team's player-manager-mummy. First the Tracy brothers complained of an attempt to sway the ref when one of the nippy little Alien wingers suckered onto the official's face. Only when his stomach popped open in injury time did the further question of illegal substitution raise its ugly newborn head.

In the final seconds of a bad-tempered tie, Lady Penelope overcame her ham-string hang-ups to boot the alien bitch into space with her secret face-compact freight transporter. Yesss, m'lady! 5-4-3-2-1-nil!! Thunderbirds are go!!!-ing in the hat for the next round. Not for the first time, the F.A.B. lads of Tracy Island *done good* . . .

How it All Began: the Facts

Ten different people will give you ten different answers if you ask them how football began. Rugby players, Italian fertility rites, Venusian warlords, ancient Chinese emperors; all these and more have been credited with the game's invention. But THE TREASURY has no axe to grind so here, without fear or favour, is the definitive guide to the birth of the galaxy's favourite game.

AGES AND AGES AGO, before television and sponsorship and space travel and synthetic fibres, lived rulers of England called 'kings'. Some of them wanted all the poor people who lived in holes in fields to be happy. Others didn't. The ones who did thought it was good for these poor people to kick things, get drunk, be in teams and roll in mud. These kings positively encouraged the poor to play. In fact, if you were poor and refused to play because, say, your knee was sore or you had a bad chest, then special bands of men with billowy knee-length pants and pointy beards would come to your house, slay your pets and drag you to the market square, where other poor people would throw hard things at your face until it bled, or until you agreed to play, whichever came sooner. This was called a 'press gang'. Poor people who still refused to play were sent to a place called 'Australia', which is Olde Englishe Speke for 'without feet for kicking'. Australians then invented 'cricket' (don't ask) to get back at the English.

THE OTHER SORT OF KINGS – those who didn't want poor people who lived in holes in fields to be happy – made football illegal, and the same kind of stone-throwing, face-hurting punishments were handed out to players under their reigns as were handed out to non-players under the other kings. This sort of inconsistency made it difficult for the England manager to pick a settled team.

A BIT MORE RECENTLY, a Scottish man wrote a 'poem' which ended like this:

> Then strip lads and to it, though sharp be the weather,
> And if by mischance you should happen to fall,
> There are worse things in life than a tumble on heather,
> And life is itself but a game of football.

This was written so long ago that football reporters had not been invented; match reports had to rhyme or they weren't allowed. It also shows that, because English people travelled north to sell 'fur' products and because Scottish people travelled south to sell 'herring', the game crossed borders in the same way as trade.

SIR ARTHUR ... moustache wax

THIS MAN (left) was responsible for organising the first-ever international match. Sir Arthur Bowes-Cudlip was prime minister of Britain, and he knew that Scotland wanted to be all alone. In a declaration of January 1806 he declared 'a game of foote-the-balle be helde in order to ascertaine finally whether or naye the goode folke of Scotlande be freely entitlede to raise their owne taxes, muster their owne armies, electe their owne parliamente and so forthe . . .' The Scots lacked nothing in motivation and desire, but the English had each been promised 100 guineas, a butt of mead, a top-of-the-range hansom and lifetime supplies of 'Dr Pipistrel's Finest Aromatic Moustache Wax for Gentlemen'.

THE GAME, played at Culloden Park, was grotesquely one-sided and became indelibly etched on both national psyches. Amidst the carnage, however, the Scots were responsible for scoring the first-ever headed goal (right) and – under the new 'shoulder-charge' law – for breaking the collar-bone of English skipper Mr J.D.C. 'Binky' Carruthers (below right). This small consolation was achieved by one Andrew McAndrew. His feat, swiftly elevated to mythic heroism, earned him the title 'patron saint' of Scotland, St Andrew. They even named a flag after him.

THEN NOT MUCH HAPPENED for a hundred years or so. Fur and herring sellers travelled the world, spreading the gospel of football. But foreigners would hear tell of the awful slaughter at Culloden and, though they were happy enough to play each other, were too afraid to take on the mighty English. There were some World Cups – shared between Italy and Uruguay – but England was banned until the rest of the world caught up.

FOOTBALL BECAME TRULY global in 1953. A Hungarian circus arrived in London, played 20 sell-out shows on 'Clapham Common' then, flushed with success and drunk on Bull's Blood wine, challenged the awesome English to a game of football, there and then on the Common. This rare still (below) shows the primitive disarray of the English attack, with the wily, deep-lying Magyar defence ready to spring forward in quicksilver attack. The Hungarians won 6–0. The humiliated English smelt wine on their victors' breath and demanded a rematch. The cunning mid-Europeans stayed sober for the return and won it 9–1.

HUNGARY FOR SUCCESS . . . sorry England routed

HISTORY! . . . on ma heid

HISTORY! . . . Binky's collarbone goes snap

AFTER THAT it all changed. Crossbars, referees, offside, space travel; things as familiar to us now as were dripping, dubbin, horses and trees in the glory glory days of Alfie 'Ralph' Ramsey. Earth might have lost its Galactic pre-eminence now, but every time a net bulges on Trans-Tanbanbulix, every time the crowd roars on Yulla Stagar, the ghost of a poor person living in a hole in an English field stirs and quietly smiles.

[AMUSING AND PERTINENT TRAINING/ BODY-PUN HEADLINE HERE PLEASE]

ONE: WARMING UP

THEN

Drive to a windswept 'training-ground'. Change into fleecy-lined 'jog-pants'. Trot round pitch for a while. Jump occasionally, touch toes, stand on right leg while clutching left heel to left buttock. Reverse. Attempt some half-hearted groin stretches while taking the piss out of the left-back's love handles and wiping sleet from your eyes. Run a few yards to the left. Turn, run a few yards to the right. Rub your hands together and have a right good spit. Bingo, you're ready. (4/10)

NOW

Part wet-suit, part Orgasmatron, the Warm-It's a smart-kit stetching from toe to throat. It automatically senses stiff or cold muscles and emits warmth and gentle pulsing and/or rippling sensations to the affected area until its intelligent cloth reports optimum suppleness. Can be worn discreetly beneath outerwear or as a stand-alone fashion garment; Nike's 99% Sheer Pro-Heritage Gary Speed BodiGlove is currently market leader in the lucrative warm-up /sex-aid crossover niche. (8/10)

TWO: STAMINA

THEN

A vast array of choices. See those sand dunes? Run up them, then down them, then up again. For an hour or so, or till you're sick. See that church spire through the blizzard, six miles away as the crow flies? Well, run to it. And as you're no crow, you'd better use the fields. See this practice pitch? Run to that goal-line and back. And again. And again. Oh yes, and none of it would work if the little fat fella in a cap wasn't screaming abuse at you constantly. Simple as that, really. It's called running. (5/10)

NOW

Hop on your bespoke, courtesy RunSim and punch in your profile code. Takes you through prescribed routines specific to your own needs: sprints, longer runs, turns, jumps, appeals, slides, head-to-head stare-outs. Mental stamina can be worked on by plugging in a HeadChip, subjecting you to frustration, anger, disappointment, envy or whatever else is required to toughen up your upstairs portions. Most accessed HeadChip is the Le Tissier Dublin '95, which has reduced even Strubilians to tears. And Strubilians have no feelings. (8/10)

Diehard 20th-century nostalgists might think the glory days of the pre-millennium were all quilted jerkins, teams from towns, executive coach travel and 'floodlights'. Here at THE TREASURY, we know different. We know, for example, just what they used to mean by 'training'. Read our definitive THEN versus NOW guide to conditioning and fitness, then tell us if you still hanker for the days when men were men and Pluto was just a cartoon dog.

THREE: BIG MATCH PREPARATION

THEN

Man U away, tomorrow. The Boss has got the reserves in red, with orders to play like Man U. But the keeper can't throw like Schmeichel, the full-backs can't overlap, the midfield can't kick and there's no one in the reserves like Giggs or Big Eric, else they wouldn't be in the reserves, would they? Mind you, they have got a striker who's a genius for missing sitters. Apart from that, there's ten minutes of two-touch five-a-side and a little chat about 'keeping it tight for the first 20 or so'. (4/10)

NOW

Mercury Sun Spots FC away, next week. Databases ('Revies') on each opponent are downloaded for a VR-Send. Each player is sent data relevant to his game and can – from the comfort of a favourite chair – play an infinite number of games against this 'Virtual' Sun Spots FC. This way he'll know which way the keeper dives at penalties, who's weak in the air, whether inswinging corners are likely to figure much, etc. Oh, and there's a card-school and a nice quiet round of moon-golf the day before as well. (9/10)

FOUR: MOTIVATION AND PERSONAL MANAGEMENT

THEN

Choose from: 'Play like a tart again, son, you're on the list'; 'In life, lads, some people take every opportunity and others take them without realising but don't know before taking them that because, er, anyway, what was I saying? Spin off the big lad, Nigel, and look for bits and bobs on the spurt'; 'Forget your bonuses, do this for the people out there who pay your wages, do it for pride in the jersey'; 'You're all shitters! I've seen more balls on my collie, and she's a bitch.' (6/10)

NOW

You might be fed subliminal Blip-Boosts, which 'appear' for a split-second among your normal video and homescreen output: 'Compete!', say, or 'Push up!' or 'Work the Channels!'. You might be sent images of you celebrating a goal or pulling off a blinding tackle. A DreamBug behind the ear while you sleep will whisper a night's worth of positive thoughts, while more advanced civilisations will miniaturise the Gaffer and inject him into your bloodstream for the ultimate one-on-one gee-up. (9/10)

SCORES ON THE DOORS

A measly, supersonic 19/40 for the 'good' old days, and a thumping, warp-factor 34/40 for the here and now. So put that in your 'low-tar tipped cigarette' and smoke it, you unreconstructed pre-millennial nostalgists! The future is now!

In football's Golden Age, it only cost £20 to stand in the rain behind a pylon next to a nutter with a megaphone. And a cold hot-dog. And still people wrote in to so-called fanzines to complain!?! SAMMY SPACE CADET says 'Those were the days, matey . . .'

IT'S RAINING, MEN

It was Christmas in Swinging 1982, back in the Golden Age of Football when absolutely everything was fab and groovy. Needless to say, there wasn't a cloud in the sky at the QPR v Chelsea Cup sellout; so it was pretty mysterious when it began to rain on one group of privileged Speedie-spotters. Who later actually whinged about the incident in the so-called fanzine, *Nattahs In Ve Barn*.

Talk about petty, uptight squares!?! They even stopped soaking up the big match vibrations just because they were soaking up quantities of suspiciously steamy water. Tracing back the network of leaky guttering from over their heads, they followed the pipes back under the roof of the stand, to the point where they eventually disappeared into a brick wall at the back.

A few seconds' calculations, and the soggy supporters worked out what was on the other side of that brick wall. They were getting wee-weed on, direct from the gents' urinal. A small price to pay to see the legendary Clive Walker in full flight!?!

PITCHSIDE PATIOS

Out of all the football grounds in Britain, Luton's Hatters' Stadium crops up in the most away-day atrocity anecdotes passed down through the fingerpoppingly ethnic oral tradition. Listening to these unfounded tales, distorted by years of exaggeration, it almost sounds as if the hippest club in Bedfordshire was actively pursuing policies designed to cause maximum offence!?!

David Evans was the first and only chairman with such a mega-high regard for his neighbours that he effected a long-running, total ban on all away-team hooligans. Okay, so basic human rights were ignored – but only in that Streetpartidocious 1980s spirit which enabled the goodies to win World War III in the Falklands!?!

Lay the carpet on me, astro-cat!?! Next, Evans ordered one of those ankle-snapping, ping-pong bouncing prototype plastic pitches, so groovily remembered now they're all safely installed in footy museums. And along one side of his Subbuteo carpet, Evans built the most luxurious executive boxes in the history of corporate hospitality – a whole row of little pitchside holiday chalets, each with a veranda, a Martini umbrella and a barbecue, which stand to this day as testament to his expert taste and judgement.

HELL'S DELLS!?!

Ever on the lookout for the most heartwarmingly digable stories, I called up my Fan-tastic Fact-File and asked it loads of questions about Grounds for Complaint. Amazingly, the database cited Southampton's historic Dell as the most unpopular ground in history – whenever the terraces' sundry slopes, haphazard angles and strangely psychedelic seating arrangements loomed into view on *Match of the Day*, it made hundreds of armchair viewers want to honk up their ring of technicolor yawn!?!

The Fact-File's own primary scientific objection to The Dell? 'The away end was shite – the same shape as a Kraft cheese slice'!?!

RESTRICTED VIEW!?!

The back row of the pitch-level tier of West Ham's West Stand surely offered one of the most attractive restricted views of Premier action. The club always knew it fell a fraction short of Royal Box City – like looking through a giant letterbox at a 5'10"-high slot of space above the pitch – so they didn't sell the seats except in emergencies. Like when another side of the ground was being redeveloped. Like it was throughout the second half of the 1990s.

Even though they moaned in the *Boogers' Bonce* journal of psychiatric complaints, fans' eyes were opened to the fascinating amount of time the ball spent above head height in the English game (around 85% in the Hammers' case – 95% if you counted from Tony Cottee's head). The seats even offered extra free fun to regulars, who developed a kind of live-action cross-the-ball game, guessing where the ball would next plummet back into sight. The smart money was always on the spot where Iain Dowie was standing ten seconds ago!?!

HAVE A NICE DAY

About a million years ago, one Chelsea fan called 'Steve' chose to make the ten-second space scooter trip to Scarborough by primitive motor-car. 'Steve' broke down: with just a quarter of an hour till kick-off, he was still in York, 69 miles from the action. Arriving at half-time, without a ticket ('Just turn up, you'll get in no problem,' said the heartwarmingly optimistic Scar-line . . .) he found the Chelsea end chock-full . . . but, still, the Pensioners were groovily 2–0 up for the Cup!?!

Appealing to the cooler nature of a home-end ticket dude, 'Steve' was finally allowed to hop over the turnstile with 25 minutes left on the clock. Instead of complaining to a fat Conservative politician on the radio, 'Steve' should have counted his blessings – he witnessed Scarborough score three quick goals, and a Herefordocious victory against their illustrious swinging opposition!?!

TEA-CAKE TOSSER

In January 1994 the Scottish *Daily Record* carried a full-page complaint from St Mirren fan Tom Graham, who was ejected from Love Street for doing 'no more' than hurling a Tunnock's tea-cake at Falkirk chairman George Fulston. Could this possibly be the state of Scottish football, when a fan could be 'unceremoniously hustled from his seat and out of the ground' for such a minor indiscretion? And anyway, Tom was aiming not at Mr Fulston, but at Buddies' boss Jim Bone . . .

The fan's response to being let off for Attempted GBH? He intended to 'become a shareholder and take his complaints straight to the board'!?!

DUTCH ELM PARK

As admitted in a letter to *The Times* fanzine, it was once possible for a so-called football fan to fail to enjoy a visit to Reading's fascinating football heritage site. Taking a bite of his delicious 20th-century 'ham'burger at the snack-bar restaurant, West Ham moaner 'GH' discovered it was a little underdone. It was raw. And just because the chef in the Biscuitmen pinny refused to cook it, GH was square enough to brand him a 'surly arse'.

Opting to go hungry rather than give in to this sales-drive for marginally overpriced blue-hooped biscuits, GH took his place in the drizzle on Elm Park's stylishly dilapidated terraces – where he was lucky enough to stumble knee-deep into an authentic 1980s puddle of freezing water!?! And discarded raw beefburgers!?! And the pleasure was lost on him!?!

IT JUST AIN'T CRICKET . . .

Just think. So privileged were fans from the Golden Age, they actually groused as they watched the giants of the game – Eddie Colquhoun!?! – just because Sheffield United's old Bramall Lane ground had only three sides, and was wedged into the corner of a cricket pitch!?! Just think. Northampton Town even swapped their fabbily draughty, memory-packed County Ground relic with a Meccano kit they imagined was 'futuristic' . . . And in 2013 Gillingham were so blind to the grooves of history, they quit their groundshare with Kent CCC at Canterbury – all because of the authentic living oak tree co-existing on the pitch!?!

NEVER EVER GO TO LUTON

Bradford fanzine moaner 'Andy' decided to ignore the uncool vibes about Luton's chairman, their verandas, their pitch, their MP and their big-hearted Bedfordshire welcome, and *illegally* sit with his Lutonian chum in a home-designated area.

The poetic justice: Andy got hit on the head by a metallic 10p credit hurled by one of his fellow Bantam-fanciers. The groovy heartwarming footnote: after the match, he picked up a total of 89p in loose change from the floor of the stand. And treated himself to a cold hot-dog!?!

They called it . . .

'SEX'

DR SKORN, half-Vulcan, half-computer, takes a logical leap into football's hormonal history.

KEVIN KEEGAN: GOD OF LOVE

There follows an extract from an early football nostalgia document – so vital to our understanding of the times – first published in 1996: 'From *Long-Haired Lover from Liverpool* to mature managerial polo-necked playboy, the name Kevin Keegan has always been synonymous with Romance . . .' The prolifically 'kuddlesome' Newcastle manager is pictured here in his natural habitat, enticing some unsuspecting 'kutie' onto the deep-end of the discotheque dancefloor with a winning facial expression and a bottle of ready-mixed 'kock-tail'.

GIRL OF THE MATCH

The neo-neanderthal sexual attitudes of most male football fans in the 1970s are illustrated by this reverse cover from Coventry City's *Sky Blue* match-day magazine. Not content with stripping this female of her outer garments, the publishers sought to further stimulate their male readership by forcing her to dress in popular singer Bob Dylan's hat, popular singer John Lennon's sunglasses, and popular footballer Charlie George's underwear.

SKY BLUE Girl of the Match

BRIAN FAULKES
NORTHAMPTON TOWN

PETER KEARNS
LINCOLN CITY

THE ROUGH WITH THE SMOOTH

The majority of history's footballers fall into the two main male sexual character-types, namely: 1) a bit of 'rough', and 2) a bit of a 'smoothie'. A hypothetical question. Would you like to bump into Lincoln City's Peter Kearns in a dark space-station corridor? The probability of a positive response would have been approximately 0.5 if you were a sexually active human, circa 1969. A similarly disquieting probability applies to the effect of Brian Faulkes's grooming efforts: do you feel a nameless need to 'mother' the Northampton Town star?

Chelsea star Alan Birchenall takes a close look at the new football mini-dress and model Ruth Erika.

GIRLS !
You too can have this washable polyester dress, just mark the size and colour you require and send 52/9 P.O. or cheque to: PENNY MODES, PO Box 55, Oldham, Lancashire.

10	12	14	16
Red	Sky Blue	Navy Blue	Black

Name ....
Address ....

WEAK PUN ALERT!?!

Chelsea star Alan Birchenall here demonstrates a long-forgotten pre-mating ritual known as 'picking up a bird'. The male sexual response was triggered in this case by the female's failed attempt to find a washable polyester dress that fitted: they called it 'Fashion'. Later stages of the male response would typically involve chicken in a basket, social drugs and a visit to The Portable Banana dancing club. 'But hold on,' it says here in a typesize too small to properly reproduce. 'First Birch has got to swing into action and try to score *on the field!?!*'

HALL OF FAME

Z4-'Billy'-Robonicon

The 20th century may have had its Alex Jameses, Jim Baxters and Tom Boyds, but who honestly thinks that this dashing half-man, half-robot couldn't have eaten them in a space-bun like a high-protein snack? Is there any one who does not think that 'wee' Billy embodies all that is great about this moment in history?

His beginnings couldn't have been less auspicious. The grinding poverty is a matter of record; the awful bigotry of those unenlightened times perhaps less well documented. His mother, Maisy McAndrew, met his father, X3-Robonicon, while fitting him with new style-chips and flange-trickets in a routine upgrade. As X3 recuperated, the pair spent time together and realised they never wanted to part.

Society shunned them. Maisy was ostracised and branded – in the odious chipism of the day – a 'tin-opener'. X3 found the path to deserved refinements and upgrades strewn with the obstacles of ignorance and suspicion. But the fruit of their bravery and love was wee Billy, whose fight for acceptance would become a fight for freedom itself.

Billy's extraordinary gifts were obvious from an early age. 'He used to ball-boy for the seniors,' Maisy recalls. 'One day he decided that if they wanted the ball back off him, they'd have to come and get it. 'Course, they couldn't get near him.'

His swift rise through the ranks of Glasgow's newly unified team, Strathclyde PanGlobal, symbolised the old order's demise. Blessed with the guile of Dalglish, the trickery of Nicholas, Law's eye for goal and Bremner's unquenchable drive, Billy won the hearts of Strathclyde's blue-and-green army, despite the team's repeated early exits from Pan-Solar play-offs at the hands of Culignian and Lower-Lunar part-timers.

A tireless worker for charity and robust champion of the galaxy's downtrodden, the solitary blot on Billy's copy-book came when he ran riot at the Player of the Year Awards dinner in 2077. His heckling, random assaults, indecent exposure and projectile vomiting caused global disgrace and the exchange of animated VidMails between planetary Heads. The furore only abated when it emerged that his aberration had been caused by an obsessed fan. Stung by the busy star's refusal to reply personally to her torrent of bizarre e-mails, Lola McRae passed herself off as a Servo-Nurse and managed to reconfigure Billy's Personal Ethics circuitry, resulting in the Award Feast fracas.

Billy's 0.66/0.33 human/android constitution means his glorious playing days are approaching an end. But his life will not lack challenge. Parochial as it seems to some, his ambition is to reverse time-beam almost 100 years to help 'Scotland' win the 1998 'World' Cup. Such a feat would surely confirm Z4-'Billy'-Robonicon as Earth football's first true Immortal.

Another Goal, Another Planet . . .

Synthesiser Soccer Cyborg GARY NUMAN's guide to Futurism in Football

Greetings, Earthlings.

You all know me, Gary Numan, the famous, mysterious recording artiste and celebrity showbiz football fan. I am rich and successful beyond your wildest dreams. I bet you are hanging keenly on my every word.

If only they could see me now, those people on Radio 1 and in the music press who sneered at my synthesiser music, my home-life with mother and my keen interest in light aircraft and leather catsuits. They dared to laugh at my frightening imagery and my beloved Cambridge United. They said it was 'ironic' that I was a Futurist. Ha! 100 years on, my visionary swirling keyboard sounds are still topping the Hit Parade, and United are flying high in the Nationwide League Second Division. I was right and they were all wrong. In the future, everyone will be a Futurist!

Oh, yes. Here is my authoritative and well-respected 'Music And Football' playlist thingy.

NUMAN THE HUMAN

DALEK'S ball!

England 1970 World Cup Squad: *Back Home* (Pye)

You all know I am a Conservative voter and very much a patriot, so don't expect a bad word about this super jingoistic anthem. Fact fans should note the baritone presence of England sponge-man Les Cocker, the first of three generations of Cockers to top the chart (Joe Cocker was a hippy and Jarvis Cocker was the singer out of Pulp and I hereby accuse him of attempting to steal my moody and magnificent stage-act).

On 'The World Beaters Sing The World Beaters' LP, Brian Labone and Francis Lee duet on 'Lovey Dovey' - we are invited to picture them 'letting their hair down on this 'bubblegum' song'. 'Cinammon Stick' is another classic of its type - 'Your actual reggae music with Gordon Banks in true Caribbean form . . .' + + + + +

Kajagoogoo: *Too Shy* (Arista 1980)

My great showbiz celebrity chum Limahl used to be singer with the New Romantically-tinged Kajagoogoo. I have put him in my article because I want to, and I am in charge around here. + + + + +

Chelsea FC: *Blue Is The Colour* (Penny Farthing 1972)

Speaking as a futurist with the soubriquet 'The Man In Black' who has recently graduated to the League list of referees and who was into stark household furnishings long before most people, I must agree to disagree with Chelsea FC. My fellow official and oldest and dearest big celebrity buddy Alvin Stardust adds yet more grist to my doom-laden yet erotically charged mill: The Colour, most assuredly, is Black! +

LIMAHL and THE LAWMAN
Take Turns in Fluffy Barnet Shock!

The Fox Five: *This Is The Season For Us* (Vaguely Anal 1974)

Still cranked out on match-day to this day on Radio Leicester, this proto-futurist classic featured City stars Jon Sammels (git), Dennis Rofe (drums), Steve Earle and Alan Birchenall (vocs) and Keith Weller (synthesiser). The wah-wah guitar is rather too 'funky' to be sulky, but Weller's groundbreaking electronic backdrop is inspirational. It brings to mind concrete skyscrapers, android's tears and controversial last-minute penalties. + + + +

John Holsgrove: *Wolverhampton Wanderers*

Wolves' lanky £18,000 wing-half John Holsgrove never tasted pop stardom because he was into 'folk' music, which was actually designed to be old-fashioned! He should have taken a leaf out of my book and learnt the synth if he wanted to be really street and avant-garde and have tons of screaming kids at his gigs - some of them so fanatical they would even shave back their hairline to more closely resemble me. Er, him. + +

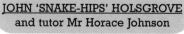

JOHN 'SNAKE-HIPS' HOLSGROVE
and tutor Mr Horace Johnson

Visage: *Fade To Grey* (Polydor 1980)

When Steve Strange started wearing make-up and making bleak computer pop in 1980, I had already been at it for two years. For a futurist, he was a bit of a Johnny-Come-Lately. Also, he was a mad keen Preston fan and that year United saw them off 3-0 at the Abbey. Alan Biley blasted a brace, and subsequently sold his hairdo to my dear showbiz pal Limahl out of Kajagoogoo. +

WEST BROMWICH

LAURIE CUNNINGHAM

Scotland 1974 World Cup Squad: *Easy, Easy* (Polydor)

I really like this because it really boogies out (a bit like 'Cars' by me), courtesy of the Bay City Rollers, and in parts there is a synthesiser in the background. The lyrics are not quite my cup of tea, mysteriously speaking: 'Yabba-dabba-doo we support the boys in blue' has a potentially moody tone, but 'Ring-a-ding-a-ding there goes Willie on the wing' is just plain silly. My close showbiz celebrity associates Lulu and Rod Stewart appear on the smashing LP. Lulu does 'Shout'. + + + +

SNOOP BAGGY DOGG
bangin' 'em in gangsta-style

Snoop Doggy Dogg: *Doggystyle* (Death Row 1993)

Once again, a little too 'funky' for these robotically-trained ears. All very well, I'm sure, in the streets of Mr. Dogg's native West Bromwich, but not in my starkly decorated bedroom, thanks all the same! I am not sure what my mother would think if I were to bring out a record which included cursing and making disrespectful references to her in the lyrics. Limahl's verdict: *Ooh to be Ah.* + +

Andy Cameron: *Ally's Tartan Army* (Klub 1978)

I detect a distinct lack of futuristic vision in this Scotland 1978 World Cup release: for a start, there are hardly any references to machines or loneliness although I was showing the way in the charts at this time. And the lyricist was clearly someone other than my very favourite future-related lottery celebrity Mystic Meg: 'We're on the march with Ally's army / We're going to the Argentine / And we'll really shake 'em up when we win the World Cup / Oh, Scotland are the greatest fitba team' indeed . . . + + +

THE NUMANOMETER	
The Pleasure Principle	+ + + + +
Love Needs No Disguise	+ + +
Are 'Friends' Electric?	+ + +
Me, I Disconnect From You	+ +
I Die: You Die	+

However passing your interest in football or history, the name 'Eric Cantona' is likely to mean something to you. At THE TREASURY we've unearthed an amazing find: badly burnt fragments of the great maverick's legendary 1998 manuscript, long assumed destroyed when its Publishers' HQ burnt down in the Great Fire of Edinburgh in 1999. Here we print all that remains of the near-mythical work, believed lost for almost a hundred years.

ERIC CANTONA's
'My Life, My Love, My Soul'

like a butterfly, a beautiful purple butterfly, brushing but barely the dew-kissed leaves with fragile wings. But a butterfly like no other. A butterfly with teeth. Teeth of pointy glass. And also Mr Wilkinson; strong like a farmer, and proud, but *petit-bourgeois*, making paupers of princes and paste out of diamonds. Crushing the wings of beautiful butterflies.

Sole surviving fragment from section simply entitled 'The Ball'

a perfect sphere, an achieved rotundity. The orb. The earth. Eh bien, the love of my life. For where else is perfection? In the mind of the artist? Maybe. On the canvas? *Mais non, jamais*. The ball: to caress, to dance with, to seduce. The ball is she. I coax her. Bring her the liver of a fattened goose. And the ball, she is mine. To do with what I will.

the heart of all men. Not only blood, not only love, but also fire. A volcano. It simmers, it waits, it spits, *et enfin*, it erupts. Does the man standing at the crater's edge, peering into the infernal abyss of lava and ash, does such a man then complain as a child if he is engulfed and borne away on tongues of flame? *Pas du tout.* I say only this. To stir the hot coals of my heart is to stand too close to the crater's rim. You made me erect fences, build a fortress, protect the fragility of my heat and my heart. (In English, nearly the same, you see. In language is *vérité*.) But if you try to overwhelm my defences, *faites attention!*

Separate fragments from a section entitled 'My Friends'

LEE CHAPMAN
Ah, Shappy. The ordinary men know nothing of him. The English yeoman, they say. A man, they say, who slept in his big comfy bed all through that fine sunny morning when *Dieu* gave to man the gift of finesse. *Au contraire*, I say. A lover of fine wine, of good music, of the rarer arts, of discourse. A man of distinction. No buffoon will remain for long in the same room with Eric Cantona and speak ill of this man. Such a buffoon, I take to task. I box his ears. Shappy helped me. Gave me many things. Gave me the

A LEAF OUT OF *History's Book*

GIGGSY
One fine day he is the corn, and I the sun to ripen him, to bring him fully to golden fruit. And yet, on another day, he is the nourishing rain that waters my roots. Makes me strong. Binds me fast to the wet Northern earth. Sometimes my brother, sometimes my friend. In him also I glimpse the raven-haired, black-eyed gipsy I see reflected in clear pools on summer days. When he runs, like a swift young mustang from Persia, his mane in the wind, defenders trailing, I smell freedom.

MR FERGUSON
Mon ami (in French, so very much like *mon amour*). He has seen my heart; naked, crimson, pulsing, wet, exposed. Yet did not shrink from taking it in his hands. He went to the core of my being when I believed nothing lay inside but darkness, a void. He fumbled, he persisted. He found something small, hidden, unknown and unknowable. The light-switch. *Et voila! Lumiere!*

Sole surviving fragment from section simply entitled 'Leeds'

and my sadness is that now they can never know me. Can never love me as I love them. What cannot be told cannot be made well again. Never will they understand that there is a place always in the heart of Eric Cantona where only *les choses* Leeds live. Leeds people. Leeds places. Leeds goals. It is not betrayal, my heart is big; sometimes as big as the moon. Never have I known the hatred that exists between Leeds and my lovely Manchester. It saddens me. I want to throw over the two cities a vast and lovely net, gossamer-thin but strong as steel, to bring all beneath it together as one. So they can sing and drink and eat and laugh together, tell stories, pick flowers and wrestle like strong boys. But still love. It cannot be. The heart of Eric Cantona is heavy with its burden of grief.

'To the pure footballer, the 'beautiful' goal is a joke. All goals are beautiful; beautiful shots which miss become ugly.'

'Football is like life only in this way: it ends when someone else decides, and at some point or other we all eat an orange.'

'Best, Law, Charlton; these men must mean nothing to me. He who lives only through history makes love with its dust.'

'If a chain's strength lies in the strength of its weakest link, then truly the soul of a team resides in its left-back.'

27

Go on, have a flutter on footy history with the oldest goalie in the universe.

Bumfluff Double Carpet

Early, raggedy bumfluff version of the Shilton tash, mercifully somewhat out of focus. On the back of the card, it says its owner 'seems a certainty for the 1970 World Cup'.

GOALKEEPER
PETER SHILTON
LEICESTER C.

Shilts' Form Guide: 'Stick a few bob on this tash not lasting the season out; 4–1 at Coral's seems pretty generous odds to me. And I've already put my house on me getting the World Cup job at 2–1: Banksy's past it and everybody knows old Peter Bonetti couldn't catch a cold.'

Running Total: Minus one house and three shillings.

Bet on the Villa

Following Shilton's World Cup disappointment, he goes for the next best thing and grows a complete set of Mexican facial furniture.

LEICESTER CITY
PETER SHILTON
GOAL KEEPER

Shilts' Form Guide: 'I really dig this Pancho Villa look, man. But I'd still put a couple of quid on me going for a clean-shaven look now it's the 1970s. I've got the inside track from Rodney Fern – long hair's going out of fashion, y'know. And, by the way, if I were you I'd stick a fiver on Crisp in the Grand National. My mate Willie Thorne says it's a racing cert.'

Running Total: Minus one house, seven pounds and 15 new pence. And counting . . .

Kevin Keegan's Kuddle Kolumn

One tiny heartthrob's plea to a kold and distant future: Remember Romance . . .

Hiya there in the future! It's Kevin Keegan here!

By the time you read this, KK and everything he holds dear – the Newkastle disko scene, his lovely wife Jean, playing his heart out – will be ancient history. The world will have changed beyond rekognition. And yours truly isn't konvinced it'll all be for the better.

Granted, you future footballers are probably reading this off some hi-tech komputer screen in your luxury glass dome on the moon. Probably while your robot koach puts the hoover round and fetches your tea. But Kevin Keegan is koncerned that, in a world full of long white korridors and pointy titanium bras, your hearts may sadly have become hardened to That Ole Devil Kalled Romance!

Play your football hard by all means. Kevin Keegan was always known for his on-field kommitment. But at the end of the day, you've got to remember there's more to life than klub, kountry and kash. We're talking another kind of kommitment here. The sort that leads you happily up the aisle with the girl of your dreams.

Here is Kevin Keegan pictured with his little kracker of a wife, Jean, on the happiest okkasion of his life (except for the day Liverpool won the European Kup).

Take it from KK. Don't mess about with your little lady. No way ho-zay. Wine her, dine her, treat her like she's a

million dollars. Give her a kiss and a kuddle and tell her you love her. Tie the knot ASAP.

A footballer needs his steady home base.

ROBOT PLAYERS

CHUCKY STRIKERIGHT

Man Versus Machine: the Symposium Decides

Never has such awesome chip and brain power assembled to debate football. Convened by THE TREASURY, each Symposium judges the relative merits of two players, one bio-based, one not. Footage, facts and personal testimony are analysed in depth, cases summarised and verdicts reported exclusively by THE TREASURY.

ONE: Alan Shearer v Chucky StrikeRight

CASE IN BRIEF: The Symposium heard Shearer was a turn-of-the-century striker misleadingly labelled a 'goal-machine'. Managers, players and 'pundits' bore witness to his being, in contemporary parlance, 'different class'. Possessed of stinging drives in either boot, and of a firm header, rugged frame and willing disposition, 'the boy Shearer' was found to have no significant defects. (Reference was made to his lacklustre personal demeanour, but this was ruled irrelevant to the Symposium's terms of reference.)

Chucky StrikeRight, created by PlayerCorp (US) Inc in 2039, was, in a truer sense, a goal-machine, and one blessed with uncannily similar attributes. Proponents claimed that since he came preloaded with Charmware and AnecDisks, he was a more rounded individual, so a more engaging interviewee than his fleshy rival. Again, the Symposium disallowed such evidence.

RELEVANT DATA: Both sides demonstrated high levels of goalscoring efficiency. However, Shearer's backers were unable to match the 12 pages of data testifying to StrikeRight's built-in reliability-ratios (0–8 metres: 94.9%; 9–17m: 79%; 18–25m: 68%; 25–35m: 54%; >35m: 35%). Countering this, Shearer's side said their man had an enhanced capability for 'the unexpected', to which StrikeRight's team replied that it was just such 'capabilities' that had prompted the development of chip-based players in the first place. The room was cleared, to allow a 'cooling-off' period.

CONTEXT: The Symposium heard that Shearer's achievements were greater; his Bio-ness meant that away from football he was expected to eat, defecate, procreate, recreate and relate to the physical world in a way StrikeRight did not. Strike-Right's team said the pressure on Chucky was greater precisely because goal-scoring *was* his life; if he failed at that he failed,

SHEARER . . . 'different class'

STRIKERIGHT . . . 'no kiddies'

period. At least Shearer had George Benson and golf and the kiddies. StrikeRight only had a RestPod, and a RestPod could be a lonely place. Shearer's team objected. Mechanisms did not feel loneliness; this was a ploy to elicit sympathy. StrikeRight's team then produced research claiming that chip-forms could indeed feel loneliness, as well as that horrible shivery feeling you get when you snag a toenail on wincyette. The room was cleared again.

VERDICT: The Symposium considered the case for four days. Giving due weight to the contextual evidence, they adjudicated in favour of Shearer. But they insisted the record show that, given the choice, they'd rather go for a drink with Chucky.

CHEATING

Only if you've been away on Pluto (no offence, Plutonians!) can you be ignorant of the controversies currently raging over cheating, gamesmanship and the use of gadgetry. We round up some of the more celebrated instances of modern rule-bending elsewhere in THE TREASURY, but, for the moment, let's put the whole thing into perspective. You might be surprised to learn that the late 21st century is not the first footballing era to tear its hair out over falling standards. Even 100 and more years ago, the game was littered with those who, like now, thought chivalry was what you did waiting on Pluto for the last shuttle home.

TIME-WASTING

TIME-WASTING, REF! . . . Zero-gravity style

Back when time wasn't quite the fluid, alinear concept we now know and love, games had 'beginnings', 'middles' and 'ends'. Naturally, if Team A was winning by a goal or so, it would be in its interest to prevent Team B gaining possession of the ball as the game reached its 'conclusion'.

The Leeds United team of the 1960s and '70s was often blamed for pioneering such 'keep-ball' techniques, despite the fact that European (non-British) sides were applauded for their technique when using such tactics.

LEEDS UNITED, 1974

NOT FAIR, REF! WASN'T READY!

One man's quick-thinking is another's cheating. The same Leeds United team also used to be cited for its habit of taking quick free-kicks. Nearer the end of the century, however, taking quick free-kicks was seen to epitomise nimble-wittedness, as, for instance, when England's chances of qualifying for the USA World Cup (Local) of 1994 were unhinged by a free-kick taken by Norway while Des Walker 'dissented' with the referee. Similarly, two players pretending to argue when a ploy fails, while a third takes advantage of a distracted defence, became common currency towards the end of the century.

PENALTY, REF!

Don't forget that way back when, games were still reffed by humans without the benefit of MicroVision™, AutoScan™ or Polygraph, and, while it was said they needed 'nerves of steel' for big games, what they actually came equipped with were nerves of, well, nerve.

LOVERBLE ROGUES

For this reason, some 'crowds' could influence more susceptible referees. Liverpool in the 1970s and '80s were particularly likely to gain from such human weakness. An opponent cut down in the box at 'Anfield' (Liverpool's ground) was unlikely to win a penalty unless he had a doctor's note certifying permanent disability and an armoured truck in which the ref could leave the ground. By the

same token, if a Liverpool player so much as trod on some chewing-gum within sight of goal, the famously 'amusing' Kop (a portion of Anfield) would bellow for a penalty with a single, 15,000-strong voice. Faced with such volume and hostility, many a jobsworth felt his bowels liquefy and his lips pucker automatically into a whistling peep-shape. Particularly when a game was in its last five minutes.

LEE WON PEN

One of this art's most celebrated exponents was Francis 'Franny' Lee, who, though lacking the Kop's volume to back him, would leap headlong, parallel to the ground, arms outstretched, belly braced, whenever a hostile boot so much as strayed within range of his ankles. His was an art carried to the end of the century by such revered masters of of the craft as David Ginola, Mark Hughes, Roy Keane, Hristo Stoichkov and Rudi Voller.

THEY NEVER LET US PLAY!

Cheating's not so different from war crimes, really; it's a question of who wins. So, while war crimes are necessarily 'committed' by the losing side, 'cheating' is usually something perpetrated by unlikely winners. It's often forgotten that in his early days as a 'manager' even Lord Keegan of Tyneland was partial to accusations of cheating when things went awry. Any team visiting 'St James's Park' (Newcastle United's ground) which did not throw itself headlong into cavalier, crowd-pleasing and suicidal attack would be accused by Lord KK of 'killing the game', 'not wanting to play', 'cheating the public' and generally refusing to lose.

MORE WHINE PLEASE!

Perhaps the most famous example of this was Manchester United's defeat in an FA Cup quarter-final at the then lowly Gillingham in March 1998. Manager Alex Ferguson claimed the home team had cheated by: i) watering and sanding the pitch, ii) trying 'obscenely' hard, iii) failing to lay on the stipulated strains of pot-pourri in the changing-room, iv) scoring an early goal then packing the defence (thereby 'ruining the game as a spectacle'), and v) providing 'second-rate and unbelievably pithy' half-time oranges.

So take comfort, Space Cadets, and ignore the prophets of doom who say no one cheated in the golden age and that players these days are just lawless, mercenary thugs. Cheating's as old as the game itself, it's just that nowadays we're better at it.

Computerised Vulcan soccerologist DR SKORN gets his football mistaken for a juju god on Voodoo Island.

Over a period of approximately 30 years, ending in the mid-1960s, there existed an amateur football organisation known as the Wizard Leagues. Teams in this multi-divisional, all-British network were drawn largely from schools, but included a range of other participants, from prison, robot and Army XIs to 'top first division' clubs apparently from another dimension.

Statistically, the most noteworthy aspect of the Wizard Leagues was the cyclical nature of their season, wherein hugely unlikely events would recur at approximately annual intervals. And every game played would be won with a demonstrably improbable goal for the 'goodies', scored precisely one second from full-time.

While 99.89% of league matches received zero media coverage, exceptional fixtures were analysed obsessively, on a second-to-second basis, by the picture-story media of the time. Strangely, no record exists of matches played between the opponents of the various leagues' 'flagship' teams – who, almost incredibly, never came to meet each other in either league or cup competitions.

But enough of petty historical quibbles. Let us study that recurrent and fully interchangeable 1933–66 season in detail:

MATCH 1: I BROUGHT MY BOOTS, JUST IN CASE

Little Jimmy Thompson, aged 14, is a Barnthorpe Diamonds fanatic. Consequently, he takes his football boots to their important local derby with Barnthorpe South End. Rovers' winger, 'Stinky' Armstrong, is arrested during the pre-match kickaround for minor drugs offences. Captain Billy 'Bomber' Rodgers appeals to the capacity crowd for any willing replacement. But the successful candidate *must have brought his own boots* . . .

Final score: Barnthorpe Diamonds 5 (Rodgers 4, Thompson), Barnthorpe South End 4

MATCH 2: MAGIC BOOTS

Cheeky Barnfield Prep College fourth-form captain Rodgers Minor attaches mattress springs to the soles of his boots – an illegal aid to aerial prowess, nevertheless excusable against the might of local rivals Southville School. With the scores tied at two apiece with only seconds remaining, the referee, quite coincidentally also the Southville headmaster, notices the springs and demands their removal. At  which juncture Rodgers Minor discovers his boots are endowed with magical 'Odour-Eater' insoles worn by crack Barnfield Wanderers ace 'Dead-Shot' Armstrong in the 1923 Cup final . . .

Wizard Fact: The 1923 Cup final was commonly known as the 'White Horse' final, after the public house where Wanderers planned their famous diversionary riot tactic and tamed their manly pre-match thirsts.

MATCH 3: POISONED BOOT

Quick as a flash, Notcher trapped the ball and – biff! He sent it whizzing into the net a mere fraction of a second before the referee sounded his whistle to end the game. He had scored in the nick of time, but the Castleboro' skipper lay ominously still just in front of the goal . . .

This time next season: Ken's eyes hardened as he saw the poisoned nail in the boot that had been responsible for Sam Shorter's collapse. For that nail had really been meant for himself! His mystery enemy had struck!

MATCH 4: HORSEBACK WATER POLO

The one where Sandcaster Trojans 'have' to play a series of matches against Rasbury Villa – water polo, ice-hockey, soccer on stilts and on horseback, and finally proper football: the decider. In the final seconds, Trojans' centre-forward Billy Armstrong notices the black spider tattooed on the Rasbury goalie's wrist – the sign of the sinister betting gang out to 'nobble' the result of the close-fought contest . . .

Series result: Trojans 5 rubbers, Rasbury Villa 4 conversions.

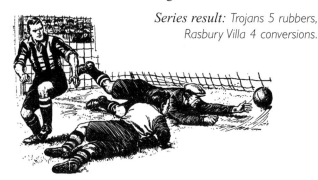

MATCH 5: IN EUROPE

Pausing only in Australia to discover a high-leaping star striker brought up by kangaroos, Kings Park Palace fly by aeroplane to Juju Island. The Kings' manly striker, Jimmy 'Dead-Shot' Booth overcomes a half-time voodoo curse, a poison blow-dart in the neck and racial prejudice to score the last-gasp clincher, marry the chief's beautiful daughter Princess Uala and settle down to a life of idyllic simplicity as a hunter-gatherer.

Final pane: . . .Until next week's vital Cup fixture away to arch-rivals WimbleArse Ravens.

MATCH 6: NAZI RADIO-CONTROLLED LEMONADE

Coalport City's manly young captain Roger 'Bomber' Booth is about to take a last-second penalty against the super-fit, almost robotically drilled team of iron-men owned by bearded German millionaire Dr Adolf Voller. 'Gott in himmel, ve shall never be defeated, English pig-dog,' the little-round-bespectacled megalomaniac chants from the directors' box. '*She* fell over. *She* fell over.' Consequently, Coalport chairman, Wing-Commander Sir Richard Attenborough, notices a suspicious radio-control transmitter on his opposite number's knee. Meanwhile, a young supporter in the crowd behind the Dynamo Oldcastle goal decides to take a drink from his bottle of lemonade. The reflection of the sun momentarily blinds 'Bomber' as he marches up to take the spot-kick . . .

Match result: Third World War avoided . . .with a 'dazzling' display from Coalport!

CUP FINAL: JUST WHO IS THAT MASKED WINGER?

Young Lord Everpool is prevented from playing football because his father, the Duke, does not consider it a 'gentlemanly' game. Not like fox-hunting, or ping-pong. Consequently, the blue-blooded youngster has to practice his ball-skills alone by torchlight – until he is spotted by elderly, kindly, almost fatherly Everpool Argyle scout Bob Hoskins. Wearing a blue velvet mask to keep his true identity a secret, the young Lord is drafted straight into the Argyle first-team for the important Cup final against local rivals Liverton Athletic. Whose secret chairman and benefactor is none other than the Duke. Who is grudgingly impressed by the masked winger's almost regal control (and last-second winner). As the Duke hands the Cup to the mysterious young hero, he almost feels he recognises him from somewhere . . .

Result: Due to a mix-up at birth, Young Lord Everpool was separated from his true parents, the kindly Mr and Mrs Scout Hoskins. The young star is thus free to play football during daylight hours – with both of his soccer-mad dads. Who see the funny side.

CLOSE-SEASON: ¡CARAMBA!

Fifty per cent of all Wizard League football teams converted directly into Wizard League cricket teams during the long, hot summer months. But not Evercastle School fifth form. They fly by aeroplane to South America for a pre-season Summer Special tour. Things go terribly wrong when the party is abducted by villagers from the sun-blistered pampas. Mr Butterworth explains to Timmy Armstrong, Booth Major and the lads: if the school team doesn't beat a crack XI of partisan bandits on a stone-strewn pitch hewn from the jungle, the outlaws will divert the flow of the river for their own evil uses, depriving the villagers' valley of its life-blood, consequently jeopardising the international corned beef market. And matron has pencilled in corned beef for tea next Wednesday . . .

Final score: 4–4, extra-time being played. Keep your eyes on that handy volcano in the background.

FAN-TASTIC FOOTY PICTURE QUIZ

Calling all telepathic readers!?! Pit your minds against the rockingly retentive retro recall of me, SAMMY SPACE CADET!?!

BERT MILLICHIP'S VELVET SACK

1. Correct. These three ace bubble-gum/cigarette cards have FA in common.

2. Correct. A whitewash; an FA press officer who has been effectively gagged by Mysteron agent Chairman Grey, and PFA dude Gordon Taylor (Blackburn) caught playing away in a Birmingham shirt.

BLACKBURN

GORDON TAYLOR

3. Unbelievable but correct. Mumbling, bumbling ex-fattie Brummie-sounding bore Graham Kelly used to play for Accrington Stanley!?!

ODD MAN OUT

4. Correct. Gary Lineker is the odd man out of these four groovy football stars from Planet Lookalike in the Fifth Dimension.
5. Correct. Quentin Tarantino, Robert de Niro and Robin Williams were all peachy keen one-dimensional movie dudes back on Earth, while Lineker was a TV pundit on Planet Carcoat.

CHEAP JIBE

6. Correct. Multi-headed butterfly monster Benny Egg-Plant plays right-half for Bury.
7. Correct. Benny Egg-Plant's big fat bottom does look a bit like Francis Lee.

DONAL MURPHY
COVENTRY

Burnley
FRANK CASPER

CRYSTAL PALACE

John Jackson
GOALKEEPER

IPSWICH

TREVOR WHYMARK

MICKEY MOUSE MANAGER

8. Korrekt. Kevin Keegan is wearing flame-red bell-bottoms with dual 27-inch cirkumference at ground-level.

9. Korrekt. Kevin Keegan has taken time out from the groovy St Tropez high-life of kocktails and kabin-kruisers to visit relatives in Disneyland.

10. Korrekt. Kevin Keegan badly needed his ten-year sabbatikal from football to recharge his psykick batteries. And after five years of hard labour at Newkastle, he thoroughly deserved a further 34-year rest-kure.

FBI ALIEN GO-GO CONSPIRACY ALERT!

11. Correct. Respected Dutch maestro Johann Cruyff has had one Oranjeboom too many, and has been tempted on stage by an enemy operative go-go dancer who looks a bit like Anita Harris.

12. Correct. Cruyff is in immediate danger of losing his trademark cool-headed dignity. Together with his underpants. And probably his mind . . .

13. Correct. You noticed the FBI agent with the dark glasses, and the sinister alien sign on the wall . . .

FOUL PLAYER

14. Correct. David Batty.
15. Correct. Faustino Asprilla.
16. Correct. Davide Ginola.

Dangerous play—indirect free kick

*Pushing — use of elbow
—direct free kick*

Feigned trip

Yo!?! How did *you* do, Mindreading
   Quiz Fan Dude???

Score 16–18: You already know how you did!?!
Score 13–15: You scored maximum points!?!
Score 9–12: With 75 most excellent bonus points thrown in
Score less than 10: for not telling my mum about that copy of *Razzle* secreted under my interstellar close-season hibernation bunk!?!

SCUM! SCUM! SCUM!

It's not very nice, is it, Space Cadets, to have that sort of abuse screamed at you? Chances are it's happened to you; and chances also are you've joined in the odd chorus yourself. Why do we all need one extra special object of loathing? It dates back much further than the Ganymede/Io antipathy we hear so much about today; to prove it, THE TREASURY wades back through the bile of ages to reveal the game's oldest, most bitter rivalries.

ONE: GLASGOW 'RANGERS' ᴠ GLASGOW 'CELTIC'

WE ARE THE PEOPLE! . . . Few teams enjoyed such a close relationship with their fans as Celtic.

History at a Glance
Glasgow was a dark, mysterious and dangerous place until the 19th century. Then ships began to be built there, and everybody had money and lightbulbs and machines made with steam and their lives were better. Their extra cash was spent mainly on sipping whisky, traditional sausages and 'heavy' beer, but so much was left over they founded not one, but two, football teams (they'd heard the English played, so wanted to learn, to avenge 1,000 years of oppression).

Why the rivalry?
Superstition was important to Glaswegians. The 'Rangers' played in blue and were 'Protestant': an ancient cult involving the worship of Dutch royalty, trade 'Unionism', and the wearing of small-brimmed black hats. 'Celtic' wore upside-down green and white stripes and were 'Catholic': also ancient, based around an elderly Italian ('Pope'), the firebrand Irish oratory of James 'Parnell' Joyce and the belief that guilt was good but could be eased by apologising weekly in a wooden kiosk ('sorry-box').

And these rituals were important?
Highly. If you practised one, the very existence of the other was a threat to your way of life. Civil wars were commonplace. In 1904, at a secret Red Cross conference in Geneva, it was decided that Rangers and Celtic would share all trophies between them. This meant that, however hard the players tried, if either looked like winning the title for more than, say, eight or nine years on the trot, directors would ensure money was wasted, opportunities lost, bad players signed or good managers sacked.

MOVE ALONG PLEASE, GENTLEMEN! . . . Fans on the terraces squeeze up to make room for new arrivals.

Did this work?
Yes and no. Trophies were subsequently shared between the sides with almost mathematical symmetry, but fans of both teams continued to goad and club each other with brutal regularity.

But wasn't Edinburgh the capital of 'Scotland'?
In theory. But Edinburgh folk preferred 'rugger' (don't ask) and tea-shops and tartan blankets. 'Fitba' was too coarse to catch on. Dundee and Aberdeen enjoyed spotlit moments but were ultimately too cold to sustain top-quality football.

And what became of Rangers and Celtic?
Glasgow was completely levelled in 2068 to prepare for construction of the still unfinished North-Hem ShuttlePort. Plaques marking the original sites of Ibrox and Celtic Park have repeatedly been vandalised with obscene nostalgist graffiti.

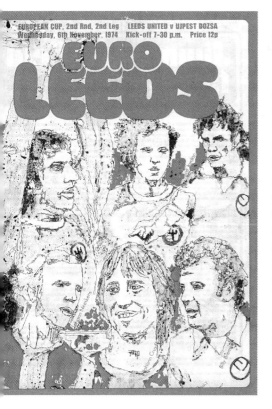

SAMMY SPACE CADET presents ten ace reasons why football programmes were skill!?!

Programmed for PLEASURE!?!

Last week's teamsheets always appeared, 100% accurate, in every match-day magazine. This provided groovy pre-match fun for True Fans, who would biro in the six changes per team in the programme they had bought to use (another issue being filed away in a fablon Space Cadets binder to be kept in pristine condition for totally chilled-out posterity).

Chairman's Message to the Boo-Boys: 'Let's all get behind the lads and pull together and maybe we'll have a cup-run. There's no money for signings, but we'll come good one day if we invest in youth (because that's cheap) and sell all our best players. Keep your nose clean, keep your head down, don't moan about the state of the team/ground/pitch/pies, and you won't get the sack from my beloved light-engineering factory which so attractively straddles the city centre.'

Top one, nice one, well sorted, chairman chum!?!

Scribbly, ink-blotty **modern art of the future** — yours to frame!?! Check out how Leeds United's award-winning artist captured an uncanny likeness of Gerd Muller (top left) in groundbreaking spidery splodges – even though Leeds were playing Ujpest Dozsa. Straight from the fridge, daddy-o!?!

Just imagine the pleasure, the personal pride and professional publicity on open offer to any small businessman of the Naughty 1990s, when it was possible to get their name on Darlington's **kit sponsorship grid** next to full-back Gary Coatsworth's shorts for a mere 15 Earth quids!?!

Join in a super 20th-century **Alien Invasion Alert** competition!?! Try and spot the four Martian fans who were drawn to this fantastic Oxford v Bolton fixture!?! Clue - look out for the tell-tale space-helmets!?!

Blown-up segments of unfamiliar city maps were reprinted for the benefit of away fans, who were well and truly sorted once they had somehow found their way to the given one-hectare square of inner city. Recommended fun-pubs, one-way systems and infamous ambush sites were not marked on **away travel maps** for entirely cool and bitchin' reasons, now sadly lost in the mists of time.

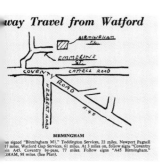

Cup-final programmes were especially skill, because they had a special, To Di For picture of the beautiful Guest of Honour on Page 3. Even before she got her head on those old coins, she was so smashingly smiley and seethruskirtocious, even the least turned-on, tuned-in fan didn't begrudge **the Queen of Tarts** their seat at a football match in which she had precisely zero interest!?!

On the back of the terracing at every ground stood a rickety little hut covered with the letters of the alphabet. **Half-time scores** corresponding to the code in the programme were hung manually next to the A-Z. Note that this double-plus-ethnic communication system was every bit as efficient as a space-helmet radio, and a good deal cheaper. Cheaper, even, than getting the PA fixed!?!

Rock-a-hula, baby!?! Hot Pennant City!?! Official club carpet-slippers, matching car-rug and flask sets, nodding dogs, toilet-roll covers, fondue sets and nice smart club blazer badges. All yours in the bitchin' old days' **Merchandise Dept**!?!

Team interviews by trivial questionnaire made it possible to find out funny nicknames and 'worst-dressed team-mates', without descending into unfair criticism of the manager, relative wage-structures, coaching methods . . . or the chairman's most excellent lady wife!?!

37

Programmed for PLEASURE!?!

British Championship? No Such Thing, Matey!?!

Here is an ass-kickingly rare programme from the 'British Championship Decider' between Rangers and Everton of 2063.

The value of this item has multiplied astronomically (to around 20 million Thatchers!?!) thanks to the glaring printing error on the cover, which gives the date of the match as 'November 27th, 1963' – some 40 years before the British Championship was even in existence!?!

Before this typographical mistake was acknowledged, certain computerised know-it-all semi-Vulcan soccerologists were uncool enough to believe the match had actually taken place in 1963, with the participating clubs simply opting to give a ludicrously overblown title to the winners of their meaningless friendly match!?!

Precision Spot-kick from the Hideous Half-back

Rather than put off the paying public with publicity pictures of their mutant team-members, it was common last century for programme illustrators to cleverly avoid the issue of certain star groovers having no head, two heads or else one rather unusual one.

Here we have examples of a West Bromwich Albion 'News and Programme' featuring the handily deformed Freddie 'Nodder' Thompson; also reprinted is a second mutant cover which offers hep-cat Space Cadets a fan-dabbi-dozie opportunity for a cheap jibe at the expense of the Newcastle United player of their choice!?!

Overexcitement at Everton!?!

Everton, you're *blowing my mind!?!* All the bodypoppingly high excitement of the Toffeemen's Golden Age is bottled and stored up for future generations in this inspirational document from the day of the League's big kick-off in 1973.

Notice how three apparently banal cover quotations were chosen so as not to show up the afternoon's entertainment in a poor light. For this was the Everton team that included not only the veteran sideway skills of Howard Kendall and the brilliantly bluff goal-blundering of Joe Royle – both soon to be revered at Goodison Park for their visionary managerial contribution to hundreds of face-saving 0–0 draws – but also Mike Bernard and Roger Kenyon!?!

The new manager leaps straight onto the offensive with big talk of professionalism, trust and respect: not for Everton fans any old propaganda about all-out goal frenzy or the employment of the club's first-ever attacking midfielder!?! The chairman leaps in with a promise of millions to be spent on international playmakers!?! And finally, team captain Kendall boldly states that he would gladly sacrifice his 'Everton

Captain of the Year' accolade for a single point gained away from home!?! Give me five, Howard!?! Give me *several!?!*

Put simply, this historic programme from Seat-Edge City represents the most fun ever to be had at Goodison Park!?!

We're Gonna Win the Cup

The age of the match-day mag is now sadly long past. And it's all thanks to this Earth v Saturn's Rings Rovers issue for the Solar System semi of 2043 – the last football programme in history.

Not content with getting their teamsheets 100% accurate (it had to happen once!?!), the time-travelling Saturnians went one better, and completely ruined the match for players and spectators: the pic on their programme cover showed the Earth XI's winning goal, a gravity-defying scissor effort by Nigel 42, notched in the third minute of injury-time!?!

Lay a bummer on me, Saturn dudes – totally out of order or what!?!

It's Us versus . . . Us!?!

This is the very football programme used by totally top science hipster Albert Einstein to prove his Theory of Relativity. Only when this match-day magazine came to the notice of the scientific establishment did they admit the possibility of time-travel at velocities beyond the speed of light. Which was good news for Edison Speak, who was covering the 1954 World Cup final that week!?!

Billed as the Irish League versus the Football League of Ireland, it wasn't until both sets of players were kicking about in the Cliftonville Stadium that the referee – a trained observer – noticed that the two teams were one and the same . . .

Not a single player (from either side) was able to pinpoint the instant when they had been momentarily gobbled up by a rent in time, but several did recall 'coming over a bit wobbly' during pre-match preparation at O'Flanagan's Bar on the Falls Road . . .

Seaside Specials

The former football clubs situated within two miles of Britain's old coastline were all nicknamed 'The Seasiders' or 'The Radioactive Jellyfish'.
Even looking through the rose-tinted goldfish-bowl visor of a Soccer Space Cadet, none of them was really very good. But only Torquay were so Not Very Good, they used to play their home fixtures on a Friday night so as to avoid any potential fixture clash with a seafront deck-chair or Cannon and Ball's fantastic variety show on the end of the pier.

In a vain attempt to make resort fixtures attractive to a wider audience, the (collectable!?!) programmes of Brighton, Blackpool, Bournemouth etc. always carried a cover shot of a seaside promenade or 'the world-famous Winter Gardens'.

And still some people say no good came of the Second Ice Age!?!

Speak like the Stars

Space Cadets – sign up now for a fan-tastic football nostalgia language course. Simply touch the authentic original star message you would like to deliver. Listen to the futuristic miniaturised computer recording, and repeat. Drop casually into conversation – wow chums and chumettes with your amazing antiquated soccer slang.

No.2:
Bubble-and-squeak like a
jolly Cockernee, my old china . . .

Greavsie on the Dole

'So I sez in me Nelson's in ve *Cawwant Ban*, you bettah sort it aht Rock 'n' Rolley or else you're ganna end ap on ve flippin' Andy Cole!'

Vocab test:
Nelson's = Column
Currant Bun = The Sun
Rock 'n' Roll = Andy Cole
Andy Cole = on the dole (soon)

JIMMY CRICKET meets Ron Atkinson in drag

'Not for me, ta. Oi nevvah tach a drop o' queer vese days. Make moin a point o' Forsyte wiv a mavvah's ruin top 'n' a packet of salt 'n' vinegar, lavverly jabberly.'

Vocab test:
Queer = ginger beer
Forsyte (Saga) = lager
Mother's ruin = gin
Salt 'n' vinegar = Gary Lineker flavoured crisps

The Case for the Defence of Stuart Pearce

'Leave it aht. Do as a favah. Gor blimey lavvadack the geezer's a foivah, ref. E's jast bottwed it an' took a tambwe in ve shirt, dinnee.'
Vocab test:
Fiver = Dickie Diver
Shirt = Dickie Dirt

'Ve bloightah's fresh aht of 'is floight o' stayahs, roight? He ahnly gahs 'n' daisy-roots it straight in ve Little Jack, roight? Ve boy snack in briwwiant, lavverly jabberly.'
Vocab test:
Flight of stairs = apples 'n' pears *or* tracksuit flares
Daisy-roots = boots
Little Jack (Horner) = in the top-hand corner, moy san.

VALERIE HARMSWORTH

Twenty-four hours is all it takes! And sometimes even the game's biggest names need a special day to go their way . . .

It was just crazy! One minute I'm handing out soya-based nibbles on a charter shuttle, next thing I've introduced the rhomboid counter-flow midfield to Neptune and I'm leading them out in the play-offs! How many girls can say that?

To think I was only working that Shuttle because Jessica's boy had mumps and we'd swapped shifts. If the poor mite hadn't come up like a pumpkin, I'd never have met the Deportivo Neptune boys, and never have overheard that crass remark about interlaced overlapping flank-liners.

It was a bit naughty, really. They do drum it into you that a ShuttleUsher never, *ever* interrupts. Privacy, privacy, privacy; that's the watchword. But I couldn't help myself. I just love football chat, so imagine how I felt, little old me, slap bang in the middle of real-life pros! Billy Hardiker (he used to be boss), was saying to his coach, 'No, no, commit your interlaced overlapping flank-liners in an inverse triangle, and the quick ball down the middle kills you.'

HMMM, LOOKS DELICIOUS! . . . *That's ShuttleUsher Val, fixing something scrummy for a lucky passenger*

Honestly, that sort of thinking makes me so cross! No wonder the game's got itself into such a pickle! So anyway, I suddenly heard myself putting him right. Imagine! 'With respect,' I said, 'you can hold the middle till you're blue in the face, but you'll never make interlaced flankliners work unless they're in a rolling rhombus.' Well! Billy Hardiker's soya-puff panda shapes fell into his lap. He smelt of complimentary whisky. 'Oh? Really?' He said in a horrid way. 'Any other tips, darling, from your long experience in the game at the top level?'

CRIKEY, LOOKS FEROCIOUS! . . . *That's 'Lady-Boss' Val, making sure the lads on the park give 110 per cent!*

He was being sarcastic, of course. Oh well, I thought, in for a penny, Val! 'Actually, yes,' I said. 'If you want the best out of Phil, switch him with Laurie and string four through the middle. Then Gary's lack of pace won't expose you to quick breaks.'

Funny thing is, I hardly gave the whole to-do a second thought (too busy!). But Deportivo lost another three on the bounce, and a month later the owner gave me a tinkle. Overheard me on the Shuttle, he said, and now Billy H was on his way out, would I consider an interview? I said if there's a creche and flexi-time in the school hols, it'd be just the ticket! And do you know? Even though my hubby walked out and my hair's completely lost its natural shine, I wouldn't swap my job with anyone!

They called it . . .

'FORTUNE'

Computerised soccerologist DR SKORN objectively questions the powers of a bloke dressed up as a big blue elephant . . .

Skill and fitness win football games. And yet this apparent truism is, in actuality, a relatively modern concept. One hundred years ago, fat and clumsy players, together with those who had spent all Friday night 'giving it the big one' at a fun-pub or discotheque, still clung to the belief that they may play some active part in a team victory. In order to facilitate such an event, these weaker players engaged in unusual behaviour patterns ('superstitions') or employed certain tokens ('charms' or 'mascots'). Thus it was hoped to gain an unfair advantage via a manipulation or harnessing of 'fortune' . . .

ROUGH LUCK

One-time Partick and Scotland goalkeeper Alan Rough practised the most complex set of pre-match rituals, all in the hope of turning in a single average performance. As part of his 'magical' routine, he would:

1. Refuse to shave on the morning of the match
2. Carry his lucky thistle key-fob
3. Take an old tennis ball with him to the ground
4. Carry in his pocket a miniature football boot he found in the back of his net (along with the ball, probably)
5. Wear his star-shaped medal
6. Use peg number 13 in the dressing-room
7. Wear under his goalie jersey the number 11 shirt he wore for his first-ever club
8. Bounce the ball off the wall three times as he went through the tunnel
9. Boot the ball into the empty goal-net as he ran out for the kickabout
10. Blow his nose as many times as possible during the match, using hankies specially tucked inside his cap.

History shows that Old Snotty-Hair could not have let in more soft goals if his lucky routine had involved playing blindfold with his hands tied behind his back.

NOT TONIGHT, ROBBIE

One of the oldest superstitions in the professional game denied a player sexual relations for days before a match. This was on the grounds that sex would leave him weak-kneed and ineffectual in the box.

But by the 1990s, a new breed of realists were questioning the old dictates. 'I think the no-sex thing before a game is shite, really,' said Liverpool's Steve McManaman. 'I know someone who had a wank two hours before a game and went out and scored three,' added hat-trick hero Robbie Fowler.

OLGA THE FOX . . . with stuffed Andrew Lloyd-Webber mascot

DON'T TELL PELE

Even the great Edson Arantes do Nascimento ('Eddie' to his millions of fans) was not immune to superstition. Having given away one of his Santos jerseys to a fan, he went off form badly the following week. He enlisted the help of a friend in knocking on some 250,000 slum-dwellings' doors to retrieve his lucky shirt. The next week, Eddie was handed back his shirt with just two minutes to kick-off, and was straight back to world-beating form. And only when his cryogenically frozen head reads The Treasury will Eddie find out that his great friend and saviour really spent his Friday night in a public house.

44

THOSE ANIMAL MEN

Wolverhampton Wanderers once wasted good money employing a man to walk about their ground wearing a 'lucky' vulpine costume, known as 'Willie Wolf'. Likewise Brighton employed Sammy Seagull, despite statistics which categorically prove their tribal totem was quite ineffective. Coventry City employed a large powder-blue elephant. No one now knows exactly why, but probability suggests the beast answered to the name 'Eric'. Astonishing video footage exists of Leicester's smirking fox-man playing pre-match 'Penalty Prize' against the local Environment City mascot. Despite having his legs pinned together in a foam-rubber trunk, Woody Tree beat Filbert Fox 5–3, already having knocked out Alan Birchenall in a qualifier.

ATTACK OF THE 50-FOOT EARWIGS

One fascinating variation on the 'cuddly creature' theme was Walsall Town's one-time mascot, Billy Bescot. According to surviving tapes of BBC Radio WM, this nightmare creation was 'a giant cockroach, or it might be some sort of mutant earwig'. This alarming insect creation of brown foam-rubber nevertheless reportedly won the hearts of Black Country locals by circling the ground, 'handing out balloons and sweets to small children'.

THE BEST OF LUCK

Here is Miss England 1968, Miss Jennifer Howe, sporting big Y-fronts and a Red Devils T-shirt in her role as Manchester United's lucky mascot. Lucky for George Best, anyway.

1946 final, County took no chances, sent their captain to a gypsy to have the curse lifted, and won 4–1.

In the early 1990s, chairman Lionel Pickering spent £10 million on a team that was unable to win at home. Or away. Fearing a recurrence of the gypsy curse, he had heather and amulets buried in the penalty-box – which began to work their 'magic' just as soon as Tommy 'Banana' Johnson was offloaded to Aston Villa . . .

OLGA THE ANAGRAM

These three people were all called John Peel, descendants of the celebrated Cumbrian huntsman John Peel, who had a song written about him in the 19th century. Young John Peel went on to continue his family's musical tradition as a disc-jockey, but not until he was all finished holding up Carlisle United's stuffed fox, Olga (a 'lucky' anagram of 'goal').

WORLD CUP WILLIES

World Cup Willie, a minimalist cartoon lion, used up all of his 'luck' when England won the World Cup of 1966. For Mexico '70, the powers-that-be equipped the drawing with a sombrero, and handed armfuls of souvenirs bearing the likeness to each member of the England squad. Peter Bonetti and Jeff Astle were said to be particularly fond of their 'Willie' lucky-charm key-fobs.

BANANA SKIN

In 1895, Derby County incurred the wrath of a group of gypsies by building their Baseball Ground on the site of their encampment. Understandably upset at the eyesore deposited in their backyard, the Romanies put a curse on the club. Over the ensuing decades, they lost four Cup semi-finals and four finals. In the

COCK AND BULL

Tottenham Hotspur's ritual loosing of a cockerel on the pitch before kick-off was banned in the 1980s, following protests from animal rights activists. The protesters had an even stronger case against Middlesbrough supporters, who would ritually unleash a goldfish from its bowl in the centre-circle.

In the 1950s, a group of acrobats known as the Atomic Boys used to entertain Blackpool fans before kick-off. A duck featured prominently in their act, and was adopted as an unofficial mascot. The duck claimed full responsibility for the the 1953 Cup final victory against Bolton, and was subsequently installed as Lord Mayor.

BAD NEWS BIRDS

At the dawn of the 1970s, Leeds manager Don Revie instigated a kit-change to all yellow, with attendant smiley badges and sock-tags. But why was the great tactician, soccer scientist and offerer of sundry bribes keen to jettison the club's traditional all-white uniform, their owl crest and 'Peacocks' nickname? Because he believed 'birds are unlucky'!

Cleaning Up Their Act

Some of the pictures featured here may disturb sensitive Space Cadets. We warn but we don't apologise. At the turn of the century, Earth's ignorance of the rate at which it was poisoning itself was — quite literally — breathtaking. Since pulling back from the abyss, we can reflect on the days which some still call 'good' and 'old', and simply wonder at how the situation was allowed to grow so dire.

IN THE MISTS OF TIME things were 'manufactured' in 'manufactories'. Trousers were spun in 'mills'. For a while, practically every northern English town had one or both of these. Bury, Rochdale, Preston, Blackburn, Bradford, Oldham, Burnley and Bolton certainly all had at least one of each, and so grew rich. But rather than club together and have one or two fabulously good teams to represent the area, they insisted on having one each and despising their nearest neighbour. And each in their own way enjoyed scraps of success. But only till about 1930.

AFTER THAT NO ONE really wanted to live in these places because all the manufactories and mills had belched smoke out of chimneys for years on end, with the result that there wasn't enough fresh air to go round and it was impossible to wear white clothes, because before 'tumble' drying, white clothes were dried on 'lines' outdoors. And because outdoors was smoky and dirty the clothes immediately became filthy, and because no one ever wore white clothes, visitors from the south thought everyone was miserable. They weren't, though, they were just prudent about laundry. But 'It's grim up North' is catchier than 'It's okay up North, but it pays to be prudent about laundry'. So it stuck.

LAST-GASP WINNER! . . . Celebrating in the inner-city smog of 20th-century Birmingham.

MEANWHILE, DOWN SOUTH, people started building cars and computers and 'services' and things that didn't involve as many chimneys. Southerners hooted with incautious laughter about the many clubs in tiny northern towns. But they failed to spot how many clubs there were in London (13 at least), and how horribly smoky and grim London itself was. The rest of the country knew. They built a 'motorway' right round the outside of it so you didn't have to go into London unless you really wanted to. And precious few really wanted to.

THAT JUST LEFT THE MIDDLE, called the 'Midlands'. But plenty dirty stuff happened there too. Cars were made in the Midlands, as were tights and shoes and bits of trains. There was so much grime in one bit of the Midlands that it was actually called the 'black country'. And just like London and the north, there were loads of clubs in the Midlands; clubs named after places that didn't really exist, like 'Bromwich', 'Wanderers', 'Aston' and 'Coventry'.

SO THE TOP, BOTTOM AND MIDDLE of the country all grew steadily nastier, smellier and filthier. (There were other places, of course, like Bristol and Exeter and Plymouth, but none of these ever had much to do with football. Not with winning, anyway.) The whole country pretty much stank. Children's teeth were made out of lead, half of London was asthmatic and weather forecasts advised old folk or people with poorly chests if it was safe to go shopping. Footballers, of course, were amongst society's fittest individuals, but even they weren't immune.

BY 2001, IT WAS OBVIOUS things would have to change. Eric Cantona couldn't shake off a nasty bout of bronchitis and retired, on medical advice, to the Haute Pyrenées. Players from designated 'high-risk' clubs were allowed to inhale strictly controlled amounts of oxygen during matches, and Ventolin Inhalers signed a lucrative deal to sponsor the Premiership. Clubs began researching the idea of relocating away from big old cities. More and more fans were watching on pay-per-view and, besides, the really big clubs reasoned that they'd fill stadiums anywhere. In 2008, Blackburn Rovers moved into the Walker-Dome on the tax-sheltered, wind-powered Isle of Man.

THE MOVE BEGAN AN AVALANCHE, particularly after players' representatives demanded written guarantees of protection from skin cancer, respiratory disorders and yeast infections. With breakthroughs in wavepower technology, the centres of gravity within the British game began shifting. For Manchester, Liverpool, Leeds, Newcastle and London, read Anglesey, Cardiganshire, Inverness, Orkney and Penzance. Only Oldham, with its Pennine location and wind-turbines, was able to prosper by staying put.

PLAYERS' WAGES ROCKETED more madly than ever as a result of back payments of danger money due after the Neville brothers' landmark legal victory in 2011, in which they successfully argued that professional football had reduced their life expectancies and that, while players' salaries were above average, no allowances for such life-curtailments had ever been factored into contracts. Also, since private cars were all but outlawed in 2010, players demanded cash equivalents for the top-of-the-range cars their predecessors had enjoyed.

FLIGHT OF THE MEGA-MOTHS! . . . Long after humans had fled toxic Rochdale, only a few super-strains of resilient insects survived.

SOME OF THE ORIGINAL SITES of historic football towns still survive. Most are strictly off-limits to visitors. Some are home to mutant strains of super-resistant life-forms which have flourished on waste gases and prospered in the absence of humans.

OUT OF SIGHT! . . . Games were poor 'spectacles' when pollution made players all but invisible.

HALL OF FAME

'X'

Take a good look at our exclusive, first-ever photo of X in action. Now ask yourself: How do you prevent it stealing in at the far post at set-pieces? What steps could you take to limit its free-ranging attacking role? And who's to stop it coming on as sub without the linesman checking its studs?

If you have answers to any of these questions, you've succeeded where some of football's finest minds failed between 2068 and 2076, when X (short for Project X) vindicated every pundit who ever insisted that athleticism was secondary to a 'good footballing brain'. X was more than that. X was a brain distilled beyond matter, a life-force, an intelligence so refined it was capable of not merely concealing itself in its surroundings but of actually *becoming* that environment.

X's intelligence was not profligate or comprehensive; it was precisely targeted on football. X didn't know three times three any more than it knew post-Chaos Theory. But if you wanted a pass to split the tightest defence or a chip over the keeper from an unfeasible distance, X was your Ultra-Matter Life Force.

Not that X's progress was ever straightforward. It came to play here when panic was growing at the influx of alien life-forms seeking Earth football's relative freedoms and rich rewards. Players like X heightened such fears. Its time at Real Antarctica was a disappointment to fans accustomed to worshipping the image of players on posters, big screens and VidMails. X's lack of recognisable presence was a huge obstacle

to popularity. Hardly anyone wanted an X on a replica shirt. How could kids copy X next day when there was nothing to copy?

X's inclusion in our Hall of Fame owes more to the splendour of its feats than to the acclaim they received. But few who saw the force of its trademark free-kicks, or the intricate course of its unstoppable dribbles, will deny X its place among the Immortals.

Had contemporary opinion been as kind, it's unlikely X would have slipped away like it did. It simply went missing and never returned. Officials and team-mates suspected nothing. Its kitbag sat in its usual spot on the shuttle, all assumed that X was alongside and quietly dozing, as was its habit. But X wasn't aboard, it had placed its bag there to buy time. Always sensitive, X had been hurt by fans' criticism of its work-rate. 'Just cos they can't see me, they think I'm not working,' it remarked after a previous defeat.

Some say X was recalled by the shadowy consortium who devised it; others that it was captured by Mercurian mafiosi keen to replicate it for criminal ends. Most think X slipped quietly away to a corner of the Universe where it wasn't as reviled and misunderstood as it was on Earth. THE TREASURY only hopes that wherever X ended up, it was appreciated for being one of the greatest footballing talents the Universe has never seen.

FAN-TASTIC FACT FILE

Calling all Space Cadets! Pull onto the hard shoulder of the info superhighway! Access The Treasury's Net-Web Database, and find out *everything there is to know* about . . .

BURNLEY

Honours: League Champions 1920–21, 1960; FA Cup 1914

Permanent optimistic status: Sleeping Giant

Famous players: Brian O'Neil (See No Evil); Fred Smith (Hear More Than A Fair Share Of Evil); Mike Buxton (Speak No Evil, But Pull A Kooky Face and Go On To Manage Scunthorpe)

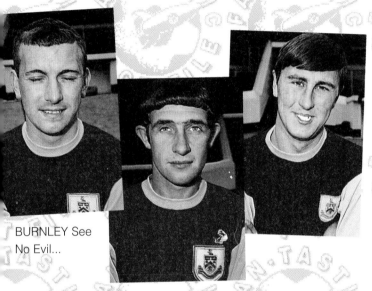

BURNLEY See No Evil...

SOUTHAMPTON

Honours: Division 3 (South) Champions 1921–22; Division 3 Champions 1959–60; Somehow fluked the FA Cup in 1976: they must have got someone crap like Man U in the final

Manager: Lawrie McMenemy

Nickname: The Stains

Kit: Red with white stains

Change kit: White with red stains

Stoopid player names: David Peach, Tony Funnell, Forbes Phillipson-Masters

Famous baldie: David Armstrong

Famous players mainly famous for playing for other clubs: Kevin Keegan, Alan Ball, Ted MacDougall

EVERTON

Church in corner of ground: Yes

Manager: Billy Bingham

Player who rhymed with 'apricot': Terry Darracott

Favourite sweet: Toffee

GOODISON PARK Spot the vicar...

WORKINGTON TOWN

Last won a League match: 1970–71

Player who sounded like a Bee-Gee: Barry Gibb

Badge: A caveman with a toilet and a litter-stick on a lawn with a slouchy Eve out of Adam and Eve. The couple are kept separate by a shield featuring a spider and a picture of famous Cumbrian huntsman/DJ John Peel. On top of that is the head off a suit of armour and a unicorn with a bunch of flowers in its mouth. With a hook on the end

WREXHAM

Ground: The Racecourse

Peter Shilton's Hot Tip: Tina's Lad each way in the 3.15

Honours: Welsh Championship 1900–date (except the years Cardiff won)

Claim to fame: The 'X' in Wrexham is interestingly one of only five in British team names. Or is it 6?

QUEEN'S PARK

History: Joined forces with Rangers in 1885 to form Queens Park Rangers

Ground: Hampden Park

Capacity: 89,621

Average attendance last season: 621

Claim to fame: Invented inter-player passing of the ball!?!

COWDENBEATH

Nickname: The Blue Brazil

BRAZIL

Nickname: The Yellow Cowdenbeath

Famous players: Pele, Socrates, Bismarck, Stalin

MILLENNIUM FEVER!

Believe it or not, some still attach huge, superstitious significance to a new century. As though moving from 2099 to 2100 were somehow more momentous than, say, from 2017 to 2018. But if you think it's weird now, you should have seen the fuss they made 100 years ago, when ALL the numbers changed.

(TONIGHT I'M GONNA PARTY LIKE IT'S) 1999

'FIFA' decided to stage a 'Festival of Football for the Millennium'. Planning didn't pass without hitches, though. Not surprisingly, it was timetabled for 1999, and, while FIFA believed the invitations had gone out ahead of schedule, they had in fact been mislaid in an out-tray, beneath a holiday brochure, an old *Marie Claire* and a sheaf of internal memos about the new pot-plant policy. Plus there'd been a 'World Cup' the year before anyway, so national teams were all still tired, sulky, smug, drunk, in uproar or finding respected ex-pros to sit on a Committee of Enquiry into the Parlous State of the National Game. Decent or popular sides had full diaries for years ahead; Uruguay thought it had a window in May 2001, but it would have meant flying in on the red-eye, playing at first light and shooting off again by noon. So everyone sent back their invites with excuses about being snowed under at work or having problems with the sitter or coming down with something they'd hate to pass on to the kids. The prestigious Havelange Cup ended up a triangular affair played in June 1999. Canada beat England on penalties. After a goalless draw with Lundy. At Selhurst Park.

THE MILLENNIAL MATCH

Top entrepreneur, TV pundit and politician, Jimmy Hill, organised for New Year's Eve itself a special game to straddle midnight's big changeover. The first half would kick-off at 23:05, so the Millennium would ring in after ten minutes of half-time. The players would emerge early from the changing-rooms, link hands round the centre circle, sing the popular folk tune 'For Harold Lang's Eyes', then throw to the crowd flowers, book tokens and wooden toys carved by poorly children. Unluckily for Hill, Sky bought the TV rights and switched the game to the previous Thursday lunchtime so it didn't clash with the Johnson's Baby Oil Bikini Kick Boxing Challenge. Luckily for Hill, this meant few were watching live when the token-toy-and-flower-tossing turned ugly; police and stewards had to separate players and fans while paramedics tended on the spot to some nasty tulip-burns and paper cuts. Hill said none of it would have happened if young people could pass the ball properly and had decent haircuts and a couple of years in the army under their belts.

SUGAR . . . Flogging his last worldly goods outside White Hart Lane

RUN FOR THE HILLS!

Something about a century's end makes people think they're going to die. Just as the crew on the *Titanic* were worried it would fall off the edge of the world on its way to China, some imagined similar carnage when the nines slipped off the calendar, as though the noughts might not turn up and there'd be a big void instead of a year. Amongst the normally hard-headed business-types banking on millennial armageddon, were:

KEN BATES of Chelsea; so sure the world would end in fiscal year 00–01 that, in a pre-apocalyptic spending-frenzy, he lured busloads of world stars to Stamford Ridge by squeezing rows of tiny noughts onto cheques. Fans were amazed and delighted, board and shareholders aghast. Bates borrowed millions, safe in the knowledge the globe would be toast before repayments fell due. By the turn of 2002 his behaviour had grown almost certifiably bizarre. Finally he was arrested at Heathrow, dragging a trunkful of weapons-grade uranium through the green channel. 'More than enough to start World War III,' said an expert witness. His defence, that he'd been freelancing for arms 'specialist' and Blues 'fan' David Mellor, was thrown out. And Chelsea had still won nothing.

ALAN SUGAR of Spurs went quite the other way. He had a prophetic dream after an ill-advised late-night snack of Bailey's and Wensleydale. His late Great Uncle Izzy appeared, told him the world would shortly end, and that anyone dying whilst fabulously rich would be harshly treated by a vengeful God. Harrowed by the dream's potency, Sugar set about flogging off his worldly goods before 31.12.99. Stunned managers received faxes from Spurs in which international first-teamers were offered for postage and packing only (with free Amstrad share options thrown in). White Hart Lane was enveloped in Winnie the Pooh gift-wrap by a top conceptual artist and given to the people of Haringey, employees' wages were doubled, fans were given cash incentives to attend and admitted free, while monies from merchandise were donated directly to Oxfam. When interviewed, Sugar said he believed a new millennium demanded new thinking, and that he was making himself meek because of biblical rules regarding earth inheritance. In May 2001 it occurred to him he'd never had a Great Uncle Izzy. He tried to sue the makers of Bailey's for his frittered millions, but couldn't afford the legal fees.

ABOVE:
HILL . . . 'Baby Oil'

RIGHT:
BATES . . . 'Bizarre'

BELOW:
MELLOR . . . 'Arms'

THE GREATEST-EVER ALL-TIME
WALES XI!

1. IDOL
2. DAI
3. STEVENS
4. BERRY
5. CHARLES
6. JONES
7. WILLIAMS
8. THOMAS
9. RUSH
10. FLYNN
11. CHAPLIN
Manager: Bobby GOULD

BODYSNATCHER INVASION ALERT! BODYSNAT INVASION ALERT! BODYSNATCHER INVASION

1. Billy IDOL
Crap Leeds goalie Billy Idol is pictured here at the top of the Hit Parade in 1964. Then one night he found a giant alien marrow in his gazebo: no more chart action for Billy. His sinister vegetable alter-ego even ditched the wild quiff for a clown hairdo. Some of these plantlike extra-terrestrials just have no taste. Or sense of timing. Or spacial awareness. Nothing to stop them collecting 50 caps as Welsh shotstopper, mind . . .

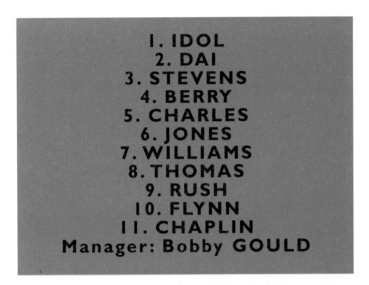
SPRAKE Idol

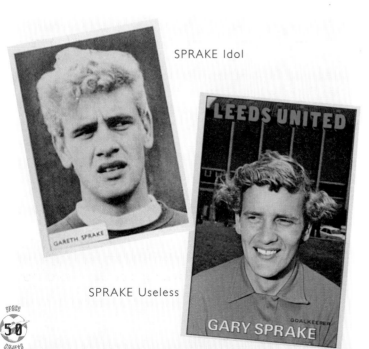
SPRAKE Useless

GARY SPRAKE

2. Lady DAI
Lady Dai, the Princess of Wales, was easily the most beautiful woman ever, with a pudding-bowl haircut that was an inspirational peak in tonsorial history. She was also the best-dressed woman ever, her expensive creations featuring bows and frills that reeked of expensive conservative taste. She was the fittest woman ever, too. And of course the sexiest. And the most loyal wife, the kindest mother, the most tireless charity-worker, the cutest blusher and the most modest all-round genius, despite her humble background as a none-too-bright Sloane Ranger. Given her eligibility and that CV, it's got to be worth sticking her in the Greatest Ever Welsh side on the assumption that she would have been the greatest natural football talent since sliced bread.

3. Shakin' STEVENS
They might have called him 'Shaky' at the back, but Fulchester United's greasy denim-clad ex-miner R&R full-back had the perfect onfield response to his critics: 'Who put the bomp in the bomp-shoo-bomp-shoo-bomp? *Eh?*'

4. George BERRY
Wales's German stopper Berry grew an afro hairdo of such impressive diameter, he was once mistaken by Patrick Moore for a second, close-orbiting moon of Earth. In his career, George successfully fielded a total of 346,000 cheap Boney M jibes.

5. John CHARLES
Known as the 'Gentle Giant' of Leeds and Juventus, Big John was never once the culprit when the girls in Land of the Giants got sellotaped to a desktop and prodded with a pencil-rubber.

NO ESCAPE! Taped down on a lab table, Steve and Valerie are helpless as the giant probes his captives.

CHARLES gives FLYNN a gentle prod with a rubber...

6. Vinnie JONES
He wasn't Welsh. He wasn't much of a footballer. Maybe boss Bobby Gould included Vinnie on the strength of his old Wimbledon connections. Or because you can't seriously pick an All-Time Welsh international team without at least one Jones. And everybody knows Tom Jones could never turn it on in away matches. He only ever really *performed*, ahem, on 'The Green Green Grass of Home' . . .

7. J.P.R. WILLIAMS

Well, Bobby Gould said he wanted a Welsh wing wizard in his All-Time XI. And he wasn't exactly spoilt for choice in *association* football history . . .

8. Mickey THOMAS

Pinched the League championship for Arsenal with a goal in the last minute of the season. Signed by his victims Liverpool in the vain hope that he might repeat the trick. Subsequently nicked for failing so miserably to fulfil his Anfield contract, and for distributing dodgy tenners.

9. Ian RUSH

Learn to speak like star striker Ian Rush in the fantastic forthcoming feature, 'Speak Like The Stars' number 4: Ian Rushairlike.

10. Brian FLYNN

It says here that 'At 5'2", Brian is the Tom Thumb of football'. But no mention of his space-shipwreck on the Land of the Giants, where John Charles was kind enough to lend him this absurdly oversize Leeds shirt.

11. Charlie CHAPLIN

Comedy genius Chaplin was spotted playing on the wing for Wales in the final years of last century. Match reports suggest he was still over-rated.

BODYSNATCHER INVASION ALERT! BODYSNAT INVASION ALERT! BODYSNATCHER INVASION

Manager: Bobby GOULD

Bobby Gould once played axeman for the miserable, drizzly, Yim-Yam relegation ghost-town of Wolverhampton, where army haircuts are Law. Proving that not all vegetable aliens are bad, Bodysnatcher Bob Hope tried to make up for the sins of his twin by turning out as heroic wing-half for Wolves' goodie-goodie Black Country neighbours, West Brom. But Evil victored over Hope. And the name of Evil's child was . . . Route One.

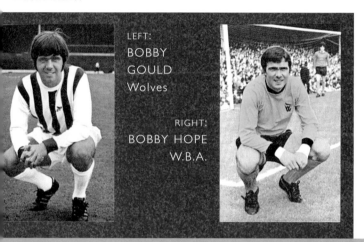

LEFT:
BOBBY
GOULD
Wolves

RIGHT:
BOBBY HOPE
W.B.A.

SECOND-ROUND HIGHLIGHTS

FOOTBALL UNIVERSE CUP 2097

DR WHO XI 2
CLOSE ENCOUNTERS 5

For just a while early doors the CE3K back four was looking a bit fragile – but then the tiny naked space aliens look pretty fragile all over at the best of times. Jon Pertwee and his sonic screwdriver failed to unlock the Hollywood lads' defence more than a couple of times, and turning around at one each was always going to be a mystical midwest mountain to climb for the Who team including so many inexperienced female assistants.

With the alien crowd making a lot of Euro-style klaxon noise in their spaceship behind the away goal, it was only a matter of time till the Time Lords crumbled. The game's best move saw one slip of an extraterrestrial lad beat Tom Baker, Paul McGann and a couple of cybermen down the right, crossing inch-perfect for late-season signing ET to rise and phone home off the post.

Who shotstopper Peter Davidson continually complained of spaceship lights shining in his eyes, but time and time again the big-headed space lads tottered down their ramp to tuck the ball home – and then off on their crowd-pleasing victory celebration of high-fives all round with their big, boney, back-lit fingers.

On this showing, CE3K manager Steve Spielberg could be going all the way this year. It's enough to make you feel all insignificant and send a characteristically treacly shiver down your spine.

Other results
ALIEN 3, TERMINATOR 2
STAR TREK: DEEP SPACE 9, BLAKE'S 7
SPACE 1999, APOLLO 13
BLUR 0, OASIS 1

EDISON SPEAK: A FOOT IN THE DOOR OF TIME

The Treasury's own door-stepping, time-travelling reporter beams back and forth through time t report live on pivotal moments in football's history . . .

Space Cadets, already they're calling this quite literally the greatest FA Cup final ever played. I talk live from beneath the legendary dreaming spires of Wembley, and you'll have to pardon my pants, as I'm still catching the breath quite simply 'taken' by the roller-coaster ride laid on by Chelsea and Leeds United.

That's right! It's 1970 and what they say is true; sometimes good guys do wear white! Cheered to the echo by thrilled fans waving hats, rattles and other homespun favours, urged on by millions in television parlours, Don Revie's plucky underdogs swept away the cold-eyed brutality of cynical Chelsea, a side with ambitions no higher than throttling the loveliness out of the game and praying for a gaffe by United's bubbly blond hero Gary 'The Cat' Sprake.

Don't imagine the Stamford Hill Hitmen didn't try every trick in the book, the one called *How to Spoil Everything for Everyone*. Spiteful comments were made behind the ref's back, personal property threatened and, more than once, small missiles of spit landed near the blameless boots of plucky northern men.

Upset but unbowed, these white 'roses' refused to be 'pruned' by the ugly secateurs of Ron 'Chopper' Osgood, Harry 'Roger' Webb and John 'Jack' Dempsey. Play swept ceaselessly from one end of Wembley's magic green carpet to the other. Back and forward, to and fro, like the tide on a beach going in, then out, then in again, only quicker.

Charlton's deadly strike was equalised by Houseman's freakish effort. The Whites again went ahead, through Jones. Bravely they clung on, Sprake's taut Welsh frame twisting into implausible shapes until Hutchinson's scrambled, hotly disputed equaliser.

In extra-time's first half Jones's fierce shot went in off the bar. Chelsea made an unsporting fuss and bullied the ref into asking his linesman's opinion. But Mr G. Todd from Rushden, Northants, sealed the moaning minnies' fate and confirmed the goal. It was all over. Or rather it was when the gallant Jones sprinted clear to 'cannon' a blistering 'ball' into the 'bag'.

With the whistle came much skipping and weeping, though manager Don Revie tried to prevent his players swapping shirts with a Chelsea team he later branded 'animals'. Rain gave way to sun, wee Billy Bremner took the cup from King George and the nation, truly 'united' in joy and warm in glee, now seems certain to elect a 'Labour' government. Your cross on the ballot form came courtesy of Edison Speak, putting my foot in the door of time and reporting live for THE TREASURY.

IT'S A FAIR CUP, GUV! . . . Even moaning cockneys know when they're beaten! Sad Blues sportingly chair Bremner around Wembley.

ROBOT PLAYERS

MEGATRON B-2-B MK III

TWO: Paul Ince v The Megatron Box-To-Box Mark III ('B-2-B')

CASE IN BRIEF: Evidence was heard that Paul Ince of West Ham, Manchester United, Inter, Arsenal, Man City and England was the prototype 'box-to-boxer' on whom many 21st-century midfield mechanisms were modelled. Competitive, gritty and fit, Ince wasn't at all keen on referees or opponents, so attracting adjectives like 'inspirational' and 'competitive'. The Symposium heard extensive evidence of his competitiveness. 'He hated losing,' said one ex-team-mate, 'even at cards. Plus he was very gritty. Competitive, you might say.'

The Symposium then heard that the B-2-B Mark III was, and still is, considered a design gem, a paragon; like the VW 'Beatle' or the classic K-Tel 'FluffAway'. Swift, user-friendly and low-cost, its big advantage over both Ince and the Mark II model was its adaptability to all conditions, and the advent of the breakthrough HumbleChip. B-2-B's side also countered the Ince corner's boasts about his 'great little engine', claiming such a phrase used in connection with a Bio-form was tantamount to perjury. The Symposium intervened, professed knowledge of antique colloquialisms and allowed it to stand, with objections duly noted.

INCE . . . 'Competitive'

RELEVANT DATA: The Ince team produced evidence that the worth of a midfield 'up-and-downer' could not be proved by data alone. Goals scored define goalscorers and saves make keepers, but Ince's value, they said, transcended statistics. They reminded the Symposium of Ince's supreme fitness and competitiveness, for which they were cautioned that no further mention be made of these qualities. B-2-B's side's case was that Ince was raw material for their creation, not its blueprint. On top of the basic model, they had developed in B-2-B the abilities to pass imaginatively and beat opponents with sleight of foot. Such abilities, they insisted, were crucial to any player seeking to be a 'complete midfielder'. Ince's team said that no one ever called B-2-B 'the Guv'nor'.

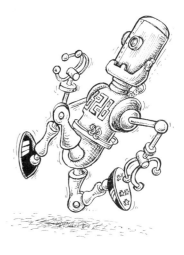

B-2-B . . . 'Like the FluffAway'

CONTEXT: Ince's backers said it was a slur to suggest B-2-B was an improvement on their boy. Machines could replicate and refine, but the original is by definition the best. This was rebutted by the opposition's reference to System 9's New Model DeanePole, the most effective target 'man' of recent times. Surely Ince's side didn't claim the prototype was superior to this model just by virtue of having been in existence first? Ince's side reminded the Symposium of their man's 'unquenchable will to win'. For this they received an official rebuke.

VERDICT: The Symposium came down quickly on the side of B-2-B, but added that, on the basis of what they'd heard, they were quite sure Ince would be an absolute little devil to beat in a game of, say, Cluedo or Snap.

WHATEVER HAPPENED TO . . .

* Stereophonically enhanced and right-to-left relateralised for the greater enjoyment of left-handed and Jovian readers.

Matthew Le Tissier*

SPACE CADET MERCHANDISE DEPT

Calling all Space Cadets!?! Hand over your pocket-credits now!?! And you too can be as stylish and skilful in space as me, SAMMY SPACE CADET . . .

OFFICIAL SKY-BLUES NOSTALGIA CAR-COAT

Back in the Golden Age of Football, when bri-nylon fashion was fab and groovy, Coventry City car-coats and kipper ties were absolutely all the rage!?! Now you can be a face in the cool scene with one of our replica Sky-Blue anoraks – as modelled here by Jimmy Zxkzxkzkx and Feargal Sharkey out of the Undertones!?!

You too can be as cool as a crocodile sandwich!?! One that's just been taken out of the fridge!?! And make it snappy, daddy-o!?!

A must for those parky space scooter away trips at only £3.00, £3.50 and £5.25 new pence.

OFFICIAL SPACE CADET HOVER-SHORTS

You've been tackled for the last time, matey!?! You're hotter in the air than a Bzagian Ormo-dragon!?! And those pesky unhip offside traps are strictly grandad's hang-up . . . when you're wearing a pair of official jet-propelled HeadMaster hover-shorts!?! These supersonic strides give a whole new meaning to 'goal-hanging'!?!

Just £7 million (+ £200,000 p+p) . . . and you're Lord of the Box.

OFFICIAL SPACE CADET X-RAY SPEX

Scientific optical principle really works!?! Look at that Space Cadette. Is that really her bottom you see thru her space-suit? Specs have no practical use on the football field – but when you can see Gloria Lestefan's pants, who's playing football!?!

$1.00 + 15c postage and handling. NY State residents please add 2% sales tax.

OFFICIAL 'STEVE BRUCE' SECRET SPY SCOPE

Pen Size—Clips On Your Pocket-6-Power Magnifier. This exciting new 6-power wide-field magnifier is cleverly concealed in a pen-sized pocket scope that lets you "peek" to your hearts content. So handy for Sporting Events, Counter-spying and Girl Watching. Also contains a 30-power full microscope to thrill any naturalist. Not a toy, but a real instrument. Full money back guarantee if not delighted. Only $2.98.
Item No. F59 $2.98

Are you close to the end of your playing career? Finding yourself with ever more time on your hands? Why not leave the footy to the Junior Cadets, and enjoy your enforced retirement with the 'Steve Bruce' Secret Spy Scope!?! Six-power wide-field magnifier ideal for viewing sporting events (from the bench), job-searching and girl-watching!?! Wa-hay!?! It's better than playing out your twilight years in Birmingham City Reserves!?!

An inexpensive gift at a giveaway $2.98 + 15c postage and handling. NY State residents please add 2% sales tax.

OFFICIAL LEFTOVER DERBY COUNTY STUFF

We've got a job lot of super-calafragilisticexpialidociously with-it Derby County stuff going cheap – but just because it's cheap, that doesn't mean it's a load of bobbins, space chums!?! This 'Rammy' money-box is gem. And look!?! It's the very one used by chairman Lionel Pickering to keep the money in after he sold Tommy 'Banana' Johnson to Villa for twelve guinea-pig bobs, back in the glory days when balls were orange!?!

'Rammy boxes' 9/6, ladies fur hats (Eskimo or Pom types) 19/11, official club ashtrays 5/-, terylene ties 17/6. Or take the lot off our hands for 2 quids!?!

OFFICIAL SPACE CADET GOALIE SCISSORS

Netmen of the galaxy!?! Amaze your team-mates by leaning on your post calmly smoking a ciggie as an extraterrestrial volley whistles towards goal!?! Then, at the last second, make like The Fonz!?! – whip out your patent Space Cadet Goalie Scissors and make a mind-expandingly speccy stop!?! No skill required. As used by Mark Crossley of Nottingham Forest.

There's no 'catch' – yours for just £3 million + £200,000 p+p

OFFICIAL STANLEY MATTHEWS NOSTALGIA BOOTS

Include magical 'on the ball' properties that will make even the most cumbersome Alpha Centauri-forward play like Sir Stanley Matthews, probably. And he was easily the trickiest, fleet-footed-est and oldest player ever!?!

You're 'on the ball'
in Stanley Matthews Football Boots
Light, stream-lined and flexible, these modern football boots feature the latest refinements recommended by Stan himself to help soccer enthusiasts.

Stanley Matthews
FOOTBALLER OF THE YEAR
for the second time

The H.28, an entirely new light-weight boot for 1963 season. Low cut streamlined upper, red instep straps and vulcanised sole with seventeen non-slip moulded-on studs; and smart white lacings and facings.

Men's sizes. 6-11 **43/11** H.18 2-5 **33/11**

SOUTH SUBURBAN
CO-OPERATIVE SOCIETY LIMITED
99 LONDON ROAD, CROYDON AND BRANCHES

Hug that touchline in space-age vulcanised soles for just 43/11.

OFFICIAL SPACE CADET SPACE BLANKET

The super bacofoil 'Stadium' blanket is guaranteed to keep your knees toasty at those draughty winter fixtures on Pluto. Even if you will look a bit of a plonker. The O/S 'Sportsman' blanket is ideal for wrapping up your larger, elder team-members on the sub's bench. As used by Steve Bruce!?!

Only 20/-, 45/- or 69/6, plus free!?! matching half-time flask!?! Buy several!?!

As shown TV Tomorrow's World, Blue Peter and How. Ideal for all outdoor activities.

Remarkable...

space blankets
Made in the U.S.A. from Astrolon by National Research Corporation.

SPACE "RESCUE" BLANKET
Weight: 4 ozs. Size: 56 in. x 84 in. Price 20/-.
SPACE "STADIUM" BLANKET
Weight: 8 ozs. Size: 56 in. x 39 in. Price 45/-.
SPACE "SPORTSMAN"
Weight: 11 ozs. Size 56 in. x 84 in. Price 68/6.
New wonder material, ten times warmer than wool, pound for pound. Tested and approved by sports clubs, educational authorities and the Armed Forces.

Rush your order to: Sammy Space Cadet, c/o Mr and Mrs Space Cadet, 43 Wilburton Gardens, Dometown, The Moon. Mark your envelope 'Hurrah!?! Another sucker!?!' Do not enclose credits. Make payment by Instant Inter-Universe Computer Credit Transfer, or by postal order made payable to 'Master S. Space Cadet'. Allow 28 gigaseconds for delivery.

The small print: Nostalgically Correct Space Cadets will expect their Official Space Cadet merchandise to a) bear no resemblance to the above illustrations, b) fail miserably to boost their football skills or personal charm, and c) break in the post.

They called it . . . 'SEX'

Logical soccerologist DR SKORN casts an eye – two eyes, in point of fact – over football's steamy past . . .

ANDY FEELEY: GOD OF LOVE

Much like his kontemporary Kevin Keegan, Leicester City full-back Andy Feeley was not only irresistible to his own species, *Homo Rondixonus Outofbrooksidus.* After his short playing career was over Feeley roamed the known universe, fathering sufficient offspring to populate a small planetoid. The remains of an all-female Snakebite 'n' Lovebite cult exist to this day on Cirrus Minor 457, where ex-rival hand-maidens still worship effigies featuring the charismatic defender-deity's unzipped track-suit top provocatively (lucky Andy – it is considered uniquely provocative on CM 457) gaping wide open.

SPACE-AGE HAND-MAIDENS worship at the feet of Fred Flintstone . . .

HAZARDS OF THE SEX-ACT: THE DOWIE CASE

Before the invention of vibrating robots with lawn-mowing programmes, female human beings selected a prospective mate on three key grounds: 1) income and status; 2) looks, taste in fashion, politics, sense of humour and size of scarf, and 3) if the 'wedge' was big enough, disregard point 2. Because elementary foot-to-ball co-ordination skills were rewarded excessively, players were artificially empowered to select multiple mates. Often on the same night. Sometimes during the same game of Twister. The primordial 20th-century act of sexual congress involved no test-tubes, but instead a vigorous mutual buffeting of pre-agreed body-parts – which, I contest, explains the worn-out, swollen and/or otherwise ravaged appearance of the sexual athletes in most demand.

GIRL OF THE MATCH

The neo-neolithic sexual attitudes of most male football fans in the 1970s are illustrated by this reverse cover from Coventry City's 'Sky Blue' match-day magazine. This model was pictured sitting astride a giant strip of plasticine floating in a swimming-pool. They called such photographs 'kinky', or sometimes 'specialist water-sports, guv'nor'.

SKY BLUE Girl of the Match

SIZE MATTERS

In ancient times, every individual Earth culture somehow came, quite separately, to give credence to the theory that 'size doesn't matter'. Logically, we now recognise that size does and always did matter – why else would this Liverpool supporter have knitted himself a neck-warming garment fully 1023 centimetres in length? Clearly, a big scarf brought an advantage in tribal competition, its owner probably claiming 'first pick' of the most highly-evolved potential team-mate on offer.

HALL OF FAME

Gary 'Gazza' Gascoigne

A tragi-comic hero of the late 20th century, Gazza's career was a tale of missed opportunities, brittle bones and amplified bodily functions. The boy Gascoigne served his football apprenticeship in Leicester, heart of the old 'ship'-building north-east of England. A prodigious but wayward talent, his elevation to the ranks of the first team was swift, and he made his debut against the mighty Wimbledon in 1984. Assigned to mark Vincent 'Shirley' Jones, Wimbledon's fancy-dan playmaker and midfield aesthete, young Gascoigne made an immediate impact by famously and painfully squeezing Jones's Repro-Facility (at this time still an outboard and fleshy arrangement).

Gascoigne's no-nonsense approach and goofy good looks, coupled with an ability to conjure unlikely goals from nowhere, ensured a cult following and a succession of spiralling transfer fees. Six years after his humble beginning with Leicester, the cherubic 'Housewives' Choice' cemented his place in the nation's affections by sobbing violently after missing a vital shoot-out penalty which would have taken 'England' into a World Cup (Local) final. Captivated by his guileless frailty and gormless charm, the country was briefly overwhelmed by 'Gazzamania', resulting in record sales of blond wigs, plastic comedy breasts and Walkers crisps.

Alas, fame's spotlight shone harshly on his darker side; Gazza's demise was as swift and dramatic as his rise. In a major cup final in the early 1990s, Gascoigne aimed a 'kung-fu'-style kick at an incompetent (pre-robotic) referee and dislocated a toe. Unable to recover fully, his transfer to Catalan giants Barcelona was ill-starred and unhappy. Alone and isolated but for his hard-drinking, street-fighting pal, Michelle 'Five Bellies' Lineker, Gascoigne couldn't settle, re-broke his toe in a freak pony-trekking accident, farted into various microphones, complained about missing Leicester and gained 30 pounds in weight.

Barcelona accepted a loss just to be rid of a man now seen as a dangerous liability. Gascoigne moved to Japan, whose footballing sun had yet to rise, where his bad toe, weight problems and continuing revelations about his marital life continued to plague him. He returned to Britain to play for the Rangers of Glasgow (Scotland). His England career never recovered, and his last game ended in ignominious circumstances when substituted by England manager Graham Taylor, who cited Gazza's 'inability to refuel himself properly'. Gascoigne subsequently helped Rangers to numerous domestic runners-up spots while advertising products as diverse as baby-wipes and aftershave, and hosting a popular radio show called Six Oh Six with Gazza Gascoigne. Awarded a Citizen's Knighthood by President Blair in 2019, Gascoigne is currently frozen in Cryo-Facility Euro/23x.@Hinckley, pending cures for cirrhosis, gout and Porcelain Bone Syndrome.

TAKE IT LIKE A MAN

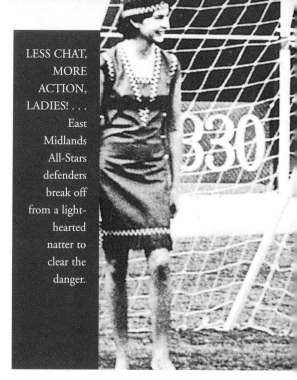

Earth used to be shockingly hung up on gender. There were men (they played football) and there were women (most of them didn't). That was it. Not a third-sexer in sight, and not much doing for women, especially for women not keen on gags about LactoPods (melons/jugs/Bristols/etc). As the philosopher wrote, sometimes you don't know how far you've travelled until you look back at the road behind you.

WHEN MEN WERE MEN

Hard, physical, frightening and tough. That was how football was seen, and woe betide any player who wasn't at least three of these things himself. Language reflected this, as shown by this interview with a manager after a bruising game in 1996:

'Yeah, the big lad's been a hero, no question. He's the one I'd want at my side if I had to go over the top and march towards guns. He'd die for this football club. Different class. Tell you what, games like that tell you a bit about your team, sort the men out from the boys, and today we've had 11 big men out there, and I'm proud of them. Some of the tackling was a bit tasty, yeah, but it's a man's game, isn't it? Contact sport, and my lot want medals for the balls they're shown.'

AND GIRLS WERE GIRLS

Anyone not up to much as a player was automatically seen as a bit feminine. There could hardly have been a worse insult:

'We've defended like women.'
'The keeper's played like a big soft tart.'
'My grandmother could have scored from there.'
'If you don't like it hard you should play hopscotch with the other girls.'
'Just handbags at ten paces, really.'*

* A comment used to describe any fight or near-fight on a football pitch. Two players squaring up, spitting, headbutting or punching were always said to resemble women flapping handbags. But fights between women captured on nightclub videos or otherwise documented were vicious affairs involving pulled hair, scratched faces and kicked shins, as well as regulation punching and biting. It's doubtful anyone using this phrase had ever seen women fight or handbags swung.

DON'T COUNT ON IT

It was almost fun to begin with. You can still read some of the first reports in contemporary 'newspapers'. How they sniggered. Abnormal levels of oestrogen in the water supply, air-borne pollutants, antibiotics and restrictive pants were conspiring to make the average sperm count in 1997 about half what it had been 30 years before. Government warnings about Pop-Tarts, tinned carrots and freeze-dried custard went unheeded. Baby boys were born minus the kind of tackle that generations had taken for granted. And what about the fish? Deformed, hermaphrodite fish were turning up in nets and science documentaries, proving to a sceptical Earth what we now take for granted: the male-female divide was beginning to

For hundreds of years me and women have talke with hushed voices abou "STRANGE PEOPLE"- men who are not men- women who are not wome No one has ever *dared* talk out in the open abo THE THIRD SEX. Is any wonder that que nicknames are used to d scribe these people?

THE TRUTH REVEALED

look sloppy and blurred. Like lipstick applied when you've had a few.

'TACHE-LASSES' AND 'TITBOYS': THE FIGHT FOR 3Ss BEGINS

Gaining acceptance throughout society was tough enough, achieving parity in the closed order of Earth football was an even taller order. For starters, what to call them? Third-sexers called themselves 3Ss, as did anyone wanting to show they weren't prejudiced. But society in general and football in particular devised harsher epithets: eachenders, score draws, stubbies, fluffies, 'tache-lasses' and 'titboys'.

'I'D LOVE TO PLAY SWEEPER TONIGHT, BUT I'M WASHING MY HAIR'

Resistance to women had lasted generations but, thanks to Pfanni, it crumbled in days. All the myths that once kept them at bay were shown to be nonsense.

– 'They can't play in the cold and mud of a British winter.'
(Sandy Dalglish scored 42 goals in her debut season for the Highland HighFives.)

– 'They're not physically strong enough, it's not prejudice, they're just not the right shape.'
(Mary-Jane Bannister and Louise Bruce paired up at the heart of the East Midlands Allstars defence in 2021. Their goals against tally was the league's lowest that season.)

– 'It's down to temperament; mentally, they're just not up to it.'
(By the end of 2053, a third of all pros were 3Ss or women; 21% of this number had been cautioned or dismissed during that season, compared with 48% of men.)

PFANNI PFILLIP: HERO OR HEROINE?

Pfanni was the first professional to be given separate changing-rooms, even though 'she' wasn't strictly a woman. Attending midwives had been unable to verify 'her' gender at birth, and it was never resolved. But what she lacked in traditional pant-portions, she made up for with strength, skill, courage and flair. A beacon of hope to a fast-growing generation of 3Ss, Pfanni made her debut for MegaMercia in 2018, and her impact was both immediate and profoundly felt in years to come.

A PFENNI FOR THEM, PFANNI! . . .
Legendary 3S Pfanni Pfillip seems less than ecstatic with her latest trophy. Looks like she can't decide which lipstick goes best with it!

Speak like the Stars

Space Cadets – sign up now for a fan-tastic football nostalgia language course. Simply touch the authentic original star message you would like to deliver. Listen to the futuristic miniaturised computer recording, and repeat. Drop casually into conversation – wow chums and chumettes with your amazing antiquated soccer slang.

1. *Get into character by dressing in a loud check double-breasted jacket (64' chest) and a simulated human hair beret.*
2. *Select yourself a suitable nickname.*
3. *Wear a minimum of 20 gold sovereign rings at all times.*
4. *Get paid an alleged £700,000 for 93 days' work at Atletico Madrid.*
5. *Ecoutez . . .*
6. *. . . et repetez.*

Champagne Charlie

'If a cup's got your name on it there's no matter how big the sideboard.'
Approximate translation: 'It all comes down to the adrenaline of the grandstand situation with both sets of lads giving it the full gun.'

Jack the Lad

'The bigger a big stopper is, the harder he can come a cropper.'
Approximate translation: 'Sometimes you've got to keep chucking it in the mixer and scrapping for the golden breadcrumbs.'

Randy Ron

'If you're jockeying one-on-one through the middle you've got to be prepared for a bit of a nibble on the blind side. Hit 'em with a spurt on the counter and knock it long in the hole.'
Approximate translation: 'At the end of the day, I'd sooner play a one-two with Maradona than with Madonna. I'm more interested in Johan Cruyff than Joan Collins, and you can quote me on that.'

El Monstro

'The big fella's looking tasty, and suddenly he's staring down the barrel of a hospital ball.'
Approximate translation: 'Give it the Row Z treatment and let's see some motorised trolley. A pro knows a coffin job when he hears the click.'

Romeo Ron

'I used to have a lot of time for Burt Lancaster, until I found out a few things about him. Thought he was a ladies' man and all that. I found out different. Had to revise my opinion of him very quickly.'
Approximate translation: 'Backs to goal and keep your stations in the narrow position.'

Flash Harry

'Play it through the channels and whip it in the panic-zone early doors.'
Approximate translation: 'Knock it deep in the corners and neg it out for pens.'

Da-Doo-Ron-Ron

'Backtrack in force, get touch-tight and they'll never pick your lock.'
Approximate translation: 'You're bossing the park, you're playing with teeth.'

Ostentatious Greedy Thicko

'I'm staying. This is the best job in the world. I must have been barmy to think about leaving.'
Approximate translation: 'Money wasn't a factor. I could have stayed at Sheffield Wednesday on a bigger contract than I have at Aston Villa . . .'

FAN-TASTIC FACT FILE

Calling all Space Cadets!?! Come in all Fact Fans!?! Access The Treasury's Infonet Database – and find out *everything there is to know* about . . .

ST JOHNSTONE
Home town: Perth.
Suggested name-change: Perth Town
Claim to fame: The only British team with a 'J' in their name. 'P's are dead common

MOULINEX Chuck it in the mixer for The Doog...

WOLVERHAMPTON WANDERERS
Ground: Moulinex
Coach: Sammy Chung
Player who sounds like him out of Butterflies: Geoffrey Palmer
Club History:
1888: Original member of the Football League, which they go on to win five times in black-and-white before crossbars are invented
1949: Win the FA Cup for the fourth and last time on jerky newsreel footage. At this point proper clubs begin to get serious and put up a bit of resistance
1954: Win a friendly match against Honved of Hungary and are hailed as 'Champions of the World'
1954–2097: Texaco Cup 1971, Sherpa Van Trophy 1992
2097 update: 16th in Nationwide One. Still 'Champions of the World'

AYR UNITED
Nickname: The Honest Men
Nearby golf course: Troon. Honest!

BARROW
Badge: A bee with an arrow up its bottom. Bee-arrow. B-arrow. Geddit?

COVENTRY CITY
Honours: Division 2 Champions 1966–67; Division 3 Champions 1963–64; Division 3 (South) Champions 1935–36
Chairman: Jimmy Hill

Manager: Joe Mercer
Badge/mascot/secretary/half-time entertainment/centre-forward: That stoopid blue elephant. And to think they turned down Lady Godiva . . .
Nickname: The Sky Browns
Kit: Chocolate with 'go-faster' coffee trim extending from jerseys to shorts, Ovaltine stockings
League position last year: One place above the relegation cut-off
England internationals: None. Ever

LIVERPOOL
Ground: Anfield. Groundshare with Stirling Albion.
Honours: Yes, including Charity Shield runners-up 1971.
Players who would never have been capped for England if they hadn't played for Liverpool: Phil Neal, Sammy Lee, someone called 'David Johnson'
Big muzzie or perm: Compulsory

PHIL NEAL

SUPER-REDS
Dopey,
Fluffy, Nutty...

GRAEME SOUNESS

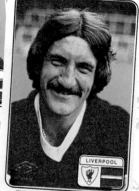

TERRY McDERMOTT

RANGERS
Nickname: Rangers or 'Gers
Famous rivals: Celtic or 'Tic

HULL CITY
Chairman: Don Robinson, AKA wrestler 'Dr Death'
Nickname: The Tigers
Badge: Tiger
Kit: Tigerskin print furry shirt, ripped black shorts, bloody stockings
Famous fans: John Alderton, Ian Carmichael, Tom Courtenay
Claim to fame: The only British team name that hasn't got any letters you can colour in

FOOTBALL UNIVERSE CUP 2097

H.G. WELLS XI 1
KOOL AND THE GANG 0

You might well ask how those sassy '70s funksters Kool and the Gang make it into the Football Universe Cup of 2097. Well, that's the glory of the Cup – the David versus Goliath challenge of the lads from the non-Leagues.

At the end of the day the Gang's solid back line of drums, synth, bass and percussion was broken down only when the Invisible Man stripped off his hallowed red-and-purple nylon to sneak in on the blind side for an 80th-minute winner.

There was no shame in the 'Ladies' Night' combo's defeat. Maybe the result was never in doubt – not if you listened to the H.G. half-back in the Time Machine, anyway. But today the lads in the spangly kit played and sang their hearts out, because this was their big day, their Cup final.

STAR WARS 1
ORIGINAL SPACE INVADERS 6

Yet another defeat for the lowly Star Wars, dumped out of the Cup at home by the horribly predictable O.S.I. attack. After the match, the Wars' diminutive international skipper R2-D2 stood by his beleaguered boss, but demonstrations on the Death Star could still spell the end for Luke Mikewalker . . .

Other results
EAST 17, HEAVEN 17 (EAST 18, HEAVEN 17 A.E.T.)
FLATBACK 4, JACKSON 5
EAST FIFE 5, FORFAR 4

Kevin Keegan's K♥ddle Kol♥mn

From Long-Haired Lover From Liverpool to mature managerial polo-necked playboy, the name Kevin Keegan was always synonymous with shared emotions . . .

Hiya there in the future! Kevin Keegan here!

I'm writing from football's distant past to tell you how the great Kevin Keegan treated his klubmates and his soul-mate the lovely Jean. He treated them both nice. With love and respekt.

Just because your klubmates from the future have got a spaceship with a lava-lamp and inflatable furniture, it doesn't mean basik human emotions have changed. It doesn't mean you kan't tell them you really like them, and give them a bit of a kiss and a kuddle when they skore. Or lay one on. And the same thing goes for my lovely wife Jean and your kute fiancée from the future with her topless dress and disposable paper pants. They're all human. Don't forget to tell them you kare.

Team outings are a great way to build klub komradeship. And it must be said Kevin Keegan very much enjoys the okkasional romantik weekend with his lovely wife Jean. Sometimes it is possible to kombine the two, like when Liverpool won the European Kup.

KK might be rekognised as king of the Newkastle klub-scene, but don't go thinking yours truly is out on the pull every night with Krissie Waddle, Baz Venison and Dave Ginola. No way hozay. We let the little ladies kome along for a bop as well. Sometimes we even invite Paul Kitson.

It's a bit like the words to that brilliant Jackson 5 slowie: 'I used to say . . . I and me . . . Now it's us . . . Now it's we.'

If people think you're nice, they give you more of the ball and you get all the kredit.

TWO: GANNIES v YO-YOS

So this is a moon thing, is it?
That's right. Ganymede and Io are Jupiter's largest moons. Ganymede's bigger and its citizens are 'Gannies' for short. If you're from Io you're known as a 'Yo-Yo'.

And they're not keen on each other?
Gannies and Yo-Yos make the old Liverpool–Man U rivalry look like two kindly vicars begging to differ over a nuance of scripture. Suckling Yo-Yos learn before crawling that Gannies are idle, arrogant, overpaid snobs; Gannies know Yo-Yos to be illiterate, shifty, philistine and dim.

So it's not just about football then?
Hardly. They've been at war on and off for hundreds of Earth years over anything and everything: mineral rights, fishing limits, cheese export quotas, poor TV reception, the use of endangered fruit in hair oil. You name it. The current truce, called in 2084, is the longest ever. The Pan-Galactic Football Federation threatened to ban both of them from all competition, *sine die*, if the fighting didn't stop.

And did it?
Not really. Now it just masquerades as football.

So there's a bit of an edge to these games then?
You might say that, in the same way you might say that Pluto's a bit nippy after dark without a cardy. After many gruesome incidents, these games are now always played on neutral Titan, one of Saturn's moons. (They toyed with staging the games on Earth's moon, but there was no atmosphere.) Xalons always ref the fixture, a pan-Galactic 'Rapid Reaction Force' (mainly Venusians and Belgians) is always on stand-by, and all those attending the march are individually screened and vetted using cutting-edge 'English FA' Crowds-U-Like SelectaWare.

And are they a treat for the neutral?
Their main redeeming factor is that Gannies and Yo-Yos don't actually have bones. Otherwise they'd be deafening.

So who watches them?
Jovians (Jupiterians, if you want to be coarse). They buy package deals to Titan and make a weekend of it. As imperial rulers of both moons, they love watching their colonial subjects batter themselves senseless. It's good, clean, family fun, no lions get hurt, and having them at each other's throats means no unsavoury uprisings or wars of independence.

What of the future?
The moons' two governors recently issued a joint communiqué which speaks of their 'sincere and heartfelt hope for new beginnings in the new millennium'. But travel agents on Jupiter report no flight availability to Titan for any weekend before 2102, and a cable station, Jupo-Two, has announced plans to start pay-per-view naked Ganny v Yo-Yo sludge-judo.

PLANET COUNCILPITCH

In space, the selection of a suitable playing area is just as important as on Earth. Some compromise may be required if your opponents are aquatic life-forms or non-oxygen-breathers – in any case, it is a good idea to check the physical nature of any alien away pitch before blasting off, so as to put in specialist training.

Generally, pitches in space are of the standard Earth type, varying only in size, rockiness and numbers of craters: not everywhere in the universe is football played on grass. For example, take note that the MoonBaseball Ground has a surface of deep mud and patchy sand; Mersonian inhabitants of Cheapjibe 7 once played on a precarious mixture of booze and cocaine, and on the distant Planet Pundit, the game is, of course, played on paper.

CAPTAIN TOMORROW

On the day before a big game, why not have a whip-round and treat your team to a mystery celebrity guest team captain from the 20th century? If, as in the recent case at Crab Nebula United, captain tomorrow turns out to be Butch 'Ray' Wilkins, simply follow their example and surgically implant a new, attack-minded brain in his big pink skull. Or just beam him back to QPR and ask for another bagsie.

MYSTERON OFFSIDE TRAP

When playing away on Mars, beware the deadly Mysteron offside trap. Beware of passing to your team-mates, too, because they will probably turn out to be sneaky Mysteron 'substitutes'.

When running through on goal, the tactical problem of playing against a tricky invisible defence soon becomes apparent: no matter how accurately your run is timed, just as the ball is about to be played through by your midfield playmaker, there are all four of the Martian back line taking a synchronised step forward and looking to the linesman with their arms in the air (Fig. 1).

The only way to avoid being caught is to tread carefully, looking out for the loose branches and grass cuttings commonly used to disguise the offside trap. Be certain to play with a deal more caution than Alan Hansen (Fig. 2) – the deadly Mysteron trap holds no threat to the indestructible ex-Liverpool armchair pundit.

Fig 1   Fig 2

GETTING A BIT TRICKSY WITH 'CAPTAIN FANTASTIC'

Marvel at the intricate ball-control skills of Manchester United's Bryan Robson. Study this valuable stop-action sequence of his masterful jinking and juggling. Observe his almost South American poise and balance. Practice these moves and add to your personal armoury of skills a) the gently cushioned instep kill, b) the thigh balance, and c) the speciality Robson reverse hokey-cokey with pike (Fig. 1).

GETTING RID WITH 'CAPTAIN FANTASTIC'

And when you're all finished with the pansy tricksy stuff, practice Getting Rid. First tee the ball up, then boot it as hard as is humanly possible in any direction away from goal (Fig. 2). Be sure and give it 100%: Safety First. Because the oppo are never going to score when the ball is in Row Z of the double-decker, Mr Flash Git Juninho . . .

TRANSFERRED THRU TIME

One of the main advantages of modern-day football over the primitive version of the game is the availability of the time- and space-transfer market. Use time-transfers to sign up players from the past who are uniquely suited to your team's needs: in recent years, match conditions

in Jupiter's soupy gravity-field have at last made Ian Ormondroyd a popular and effective striker, thanks to his exceptionally low cross-sectional area. Just last week, the Leicester Mercuries signed the 4'11", 145 m.p.h. winger Franz Carr from Aston Villa, although no one is quite sure why. And what Blackhole Rovers boss could turn down a future bid of £4.6 billion for the great David Batty, so sadly misunderstood in his own time?

Time-transfers can also be usefully employed at set-pieces. After your highly fancied left-back with a foot like a hammer has blasted his 30-yard free-kick 30 yards over the bar, send him back in time for as little as £2 million per second, and buy the big clod another chance to catch it like he did in training.

Here we see George Best (Moonchester United) taking full advantage of five simultaneous £1.5 million time-transfers to notch up a minimum of four spectacular goals (Fig. 1). QPR's Rodney Mars uses twin time-transfers to beat himself comprehensively with two separate flashes of brilliance (Fig. 2). See how he first shows virtuoso skills despite having his arms handcuffed behind his back, and then quite literally turns himself inside-out with a judicious dislocation of his left hip.

HOARDING CASH

When members of your team are pictured in futuristic skill-tip features, use available advertising space to raise money for club coffers. Here Colin Todd, Mike Channon and Gerry Francis demonstrate short, weighted passes whilst subtly implanting subliminal ads for Jovian 'DEI/DIIIIoELL' space blankets and delicious 'Io FiiAH/' snack-bars. Meanwhile, England goalie Chris Woods looks after his own interests via a special introductory offer on his personal hoarding.

MATCH ABANDONED!

A hundred years ago, before omni-roofs and ambience-control, matches would actually be 'postponed' beforehand because of 'adverse' weather conditions. But rather than gloat over the strides we've since made, let's reflect instead on some of those occasions when even technology and our heaviest brains have failed to stop the abandonment of games already in progress.

AWAY TEAM TURNS TO DUST!

Part-timers Proxima Vectra's reward for winning the Astral Qualifiers was a tough away tie at in-form Dynamo Gargox in the Pepsi Challenge 3rd round. Just staying awake after major Time Compression is too much for most, but staying fresh enough to outwit a tight sweeper system is something else. Fixture congestion back home meant Vectra had to squeeze 500 light years into just a fortnight's trip, and something went badly wrong. Dynamo skipper L/uj.7 said later: 'It was horrible. We was one up and looking to bury them, loading the box, slinging it in. I'm on the back stick, and I notice their keeper's just wrinkling up. Two more of their boys are kneeling there. Their hair's gone white and fallen out, they're screaming something rotten and all the flesh is shrivelling up off their heads till they're just skulls and that. The whole team's writhing about, howling, eyeballs and teeth all over the shop. Basically, they're fit lads one minute, but by the time we get their physio on, they're skeletons. Halfway across the pitch, wallop, he's down as well. Two minutes later we're all in the bath and the groundsman's on the pitch with a dustpan and brush. It sounds harsh, but what can you do?'

Dynamo went on to win the cup and, as a mark of respect, filled the trophy with the dusty debris of PVFC and sent it to the distant star, a fitting memorial to their ashy and stricken opponents.

Waterlogged Pitch 1,
Damzelindistrsz Dortmund 0

CONTINUUM RUPTURE SHOCK!

There was nothing remarkable about the All-Earth Alliance game in 2019 between the Tokyo Wildcats and Orkney Caledonia. The crowd was thin and the pay-per-view figures wouldn't buy a sniff of the Platinum League. The game's only strangeness was that players complained of rushing noises, dizzy spells and nose-bleeds. Tokyo veteran Robbie Fowler and Orkney skipper Gavin Strachan had to swallow continually to unblock their ears. These are, of course, classic signs of a disturbance near a fault in the space-time continuum. After an hour there was a huge ripping noise, like separating strips of mile-wide velcro, and the fault became a rupture along the halfway line. Confused and scared, players scattered, moving warily back to mid-pitch to peer into the void. To their amazement, down the hole (from which came the tell-tale fishy smell so typical of such ruptures) was clearly visible a Victorian mill-town. Officials and players stood awestruck as horses clopped along cobbled streets, bakers with mutton-chop whiskers sold barm-cakes to women in aprons, skinny girls on corners sold matches and smoke

Bury FC, late 19th century

billowed thickly from blackened chimneys. It transpired that an Orkney midfielder, Mitchell McCoist, had fallen down the chasm. He could be seen being helped to his feet and suspiciously eyed by the townsfolk below. The game was abandoned and he never returned. But team portraits of Bury FC from the late 19th century show McCoist's spitting image sitting second from the left in the front row.

DANGER! FLOATING STRIKER!

Way back in the 20th century, if a ground had a 'special atmosphere', it was noisy or fierce. But by the 2020s, the 'special atmosphere' of Virgin Orb-Stat-1 meant something quite different. Orbiting space stations were still a novelty; the game arranged to mark VOS-1's fifth anniversary in 2025 was a major event, played between Northern and Southern Hemisphere XIs. Dignitaries from all 'nations' attended, as did representatives of life-forms to whom Earth had but recently been introduced. VOS-1's pitch was top quality and fan comfort – though crude by modern standards – was state-of-the-art. But early-century scientists were a little slow on the uptake *vis-à-vis* gravity. Complex compounds of gases and carefully calibrated air-pressures were very cutting edge in pre-enlightened times. With hindsight, the prestige and success of such a huge event was too great a weight for such flimsy technology to bear. The rot had set in by the half-hour mark; NorthHem's first goal rolled tamely over the line with the SouthHem keeper floating helplessly half a metre above the ground. SouthHem's long-ball tactics rebounded as NorthHem's central defenders found themselves able to kick away easily high balls over the top. The ref's extra body-weight meant he was the only participant with his boots touching the turf by the start of the second half, and ten minutes later three players had been treated for mild concussions sustained in collision with the underside of the stadium roof. Fans had similar problems; only swift-thinking and even quicker knot-tying by the emergency services prevented a clutch of VIPs floating into orbit from the Dignitaries' Box. A family from Alloa, 'Scotland', on a once-in-a-lifetime package trip, wasn't so lucky. They were rescued a day later, three miles up and suffering from hypothermia and Weightless Fever. It was an embarrassing false start to Earth's adventure in space and and one which still inspires non-Earthly life-forms to taunt Earth-fans. ('Float in a minute! You're gonna float in a minute!'; 'We can see you, we can see you, we can see you floating out, we can see you floating out!'; 'Come and have a float if you thing you're light enough!' etc . . .)

'Three players were treated for concussion, sustained in collision with the underside of the stadium roof . . .'

Back in the days before UK United, Europe Rovers and World Wanderers, there was . . .

THE GREATEST-EVER ALL-TIME
ENGLAND XI!

1. BANKS
2. LINEKER
3. REGINA
4. BARNES
5. DARE
6. MOORE
007. BOND
8. MATTHEWS
9. MARTIN
10. LE TISSIER
11. RACE

Manager: Bryan BOBBYROBSON

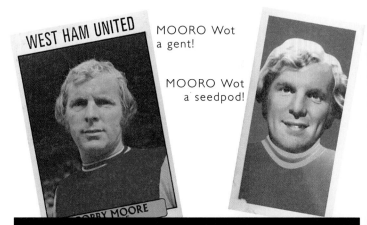

MOORO Wot a gent!

MOORO Wot a seedpod!

BODYSNATCHER INVASION ALERT! BODYSNAT INVASION ALERT! BODYSNATCHER INVASION

1. Gordon BANKS
Here is a football pun from the 20th century: Gordon Banks is a jolly good goalie, who plays for England. He is as safe as the Bank of England. Hence his nickname, 'Banks of England'.

2. George Winston LINEKER
Little George's all-time caps record (hundreds), international goalscoring record (thousands) and disciplinary record (nil) controversially get him the squad nod ahead of the England manager's job, in which capacity he was recently sainted.

3. Victoria 'Nobby' REGINA
Suffered bad press for having a TV pub and a particularly moralistic period in British history named after her, and also for her habit of removing her front teeth during play. Nicknamed 'Nobby' for her prodigious youth policy (12 at last count), Queen Vic (God bless her) was crushing in the tackle and positively fearsome on the front stick.

NOBBY STILES

QUEEN VIC
God bless her

4. John BARNES
Only joking, Barnesy.

5. Dan DARE
Included because a Pilot of the Future is bound to be pretty useful in a major international/galactic rumble. Even if his 'future' was supposed to be 1986.

6. Sir Bobby MOORE
When England was world leader in gentlemanly behaviour, mini-skirts, drugs that made you think you were a crinkle-cut chip and football, Sir Bob was famous for holding up the Planet Earth Cup. And also for those funny stretchy-leg tackles that he used to pull off like a leopard pouncing on a hapless gazelle just when people thought those Brazilian forwards were beginning to take the piss. Yet here we prove beyond reasonable doubt that Sir Bobby was the victim of alien bodysnatchers who parked one of their demon seedpods in his window-box. Overnight, Bob turned grumpy and began to harbour a secret tactical agenda to turn all right-thinking humanoids into mindless Communists. The sort of people who wouldn't notice if their head was lopped off and superimposed onto an amateurishly coloured-in West Ham kit . . .

007. James BOND
When you're up against some foreign foe intent on the destruction of 4-2-4 and the British Way of Life with a squad of purple-tracksuited high-tackling kung-fu villains, the best form of defence is often attack. The sharpshooting Jim Bond was most deadly dropped in deep behind the opposition line, where he would upset their evil tactics for world domination, soak up punishment, blow up the secret island . . . and never fail to score.

8. Sir Stanley MATTHEWS
Sir Stanley was known as the 'Wizard of the Dribble'. But that's his business. He is perhaps best remembered as easily the greatest player ever. The FA Cup Final of 1746 was known as the 'Matthews Final' because Stan Mortenson scored a hat-trick.

72

No. 9 Alvin Martin

Martin starred in the England number 9 shirt when he was young. Yet reference books suggest Martin was *never* young . . . And, stretching credibility yet further, it says here the big clod 'collected a total of 13 full England caps' . . . Only microscopic examination finally gives up a clue to suggest the card may be a cunning fake: the lettering printed across Al's 'international' jersey reads not the time-honoured 'National Breakdown', but instead 'Pacesetters Don't Smoke', a legend seemingly designed to invite derision.

10. Matthew LE TISSIER

Yes, *of course* he's in the bloody team. Only Taylor or Venables would leave him out of the England set-up, and gift *Barnes* his 150th cap. He's *in*, okay? *Forever.*

11. Roy RACE

Although irrefutable documentation exists showing the evergreen Race was captain of England from 1955–2029, any amount of cross-referencing fails to uncover additional data on his club team, Melchester Rovers. Race makes the All-Time team on the strength of his Amazing Outdated Hairdon't, which he somehow contrived to keep stalled precisely three years behind current fashions throughout his lengthy career.

9. Alvin MARTIN

According to this pictorial evidence recently unearthed for the first time in a century, geriatric West Ham clogger Alvin

---

PETER SHILTON and his Amazing Gambling 'Tash!

Go on, have a flutter on pop history with the oldest swinger in town . . .

3. 'Three Bets to Heaven'

Tarzan's running total is currently minus one house, seven pounds and 15 new pence.

Shilts' Form Guide: 'Ee, I look like a young Valentino here, me duck. A quid says that autograph's my real handwriting. Make it a fiver if you're so sure. You've got to speculate to accumulate, eh? I saw this local band last night, sort of cabaret rock 'n' roll with Dion

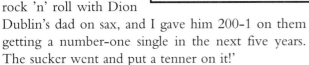

Dublin's dad on sax, and I gave him 200-1 on them getting a number-one single in the next five years. The sucker went and put a tenner on it!'

Running Total: Minus one house and £2012.15.

4. 'Side by Side'

Shilton's revived kink, earmuffs and pop-star status make him an international grooming idol of the '70s.

Shilts' Form Guide: 'Sharing the England job with Ray's costing me a packet, so we're releasing a record to cash in. Course, there's no way a bloke as popular as me, with a number-one single under his belt, could ever fall on hard times. If things got tough I'd just apply for the Leicester

manager's job. I'd put my shirt on them bending over backwards to get me back to Filbert Street.'

Running Total: The Hipster Tipster scores minus one house, minus £2012.15, minus three shirts . . . and counting.

Strange Tribal Rituals

COATES Hell toupee . . .

SCIENTIFIC PREPARATION

Participating Cup-final teams would spend their pre-match night in separate but identical Surrey hotels rated by the Automobile Association as 'swanky' (swimming-puddle, table-tennis room, pornographic televisual options). Liverpudlian squad-members left out of the following morning's team selections would consequently not feel they had entirely wasted their time. After protein-rich 'pasta' meals, gambling schools would be organised on board convergent 'luxury' buses featuring curtains and pasta-toilets. Destination: the famous twin daleks of Wembley.

LOGIC COUNT: 2/10
Like all Italian food, the taste-free wheat glue known as 'pasta' was free to produce, yet sold in hotels and restaurants at a premium price. Another Italian delicacy was 'pizza pie': cheese on toast. The addition of minimal ham and pineapple topping was wrongly supposed to make this cheese on toast Hawaiian in origin. The team could have been provided with a far more logical packed lunch.

EXAMINING THE WIDE-OPEN SPACES

Unlike before any other match, it was deemed necessary for all players to reconnoitre the 'wide-open spaces' of Wembley Stadium's playing surface, 'soaking up the atmosphere' wearing a suit and a tie with a large knot.

LOGIC COUNT: 1/10
The pitch at Wembley was of a regulation layout and size.

DEFERRED GRATIFICATION

Immediately pre-match both sets of players were forced, under military surveillance, to mime the words of a nationalist anthem. A minor member of the ruling royal family would be on hand to ensure the sportsmen did not break into renditions of their own 'jaunty' Cup-final song. During this period, when Lady Di would traditionally arrange for certain players to show further, individual proof of their servitude, 100,000 loyal subjects hid under giant bedsheets and threatened their rival fans with summary extinction.

LOGIC COUNT: 8/10
Lady Di was beautiful, and she did a lot of work for charity. Look at the alternative – a country and a Cup final overseen by a communist dictator with little piggy eyes.

THE ANTI-CLIMAX

Televisual coverage of a Cup final would feature an anal-retentive manic-obsessive periodically shouting 'Ooh, nasty', 'Timely Everton interception' and 'Shots on target' amidst a cornucopia of random, unrelated facts and statistics. The match would only be allowed to kick off once three ex-players (housed in a glass box hanging over the pitch) had all solemnly predicted the favourites would emerge as winners. The uneventful first half would be put down to 'big-match nerves'. The second half would slip into outright tedium because 'neither team wanted to lose'. A procedural competition stifled by negative tactics would at some point be described as 'two great teams cancelling each other out'.

LOGIC COUNT: 2/10
Apart from the pundits' statistically excellent predictions, TV coverage was nonsensical. In real life, no one has ever said 'dispossess' when they mean 'tackle'.

THE 39 STEPS

The eventual victors would triumphally mount the steps to Lady Di's royal box. These were the '39 Steps' referred to in the famous 1960s football thriller edited by Manchester United's Martin Buchan. Lady Di would then present the Cup to the winning team captain, who would kiss the expensive, hollow vessel and hold her up for the crowd to cheer. In anticipation of getting to dirty Di's hand, players would all too often mar the ceremony by stealing items of onlookers' clothing: Evertonian booty including scarves, bobble-hats, trousers and a diamond tiara was shown off in one famously unruly 'lap of victory' around the dog-track.

'PLENTY OF ROOM for a little one, Frannie!'

Clinical soccerologist DR SKORN studies the logic of ancient Cup Final traditions . . .

LOGIC COUNT: 0/10

Rather than make 28 men climb up and down 78 steps, wasting a total energy quantum equivalent to two overrated 'pasta-shell' meals, it would have been more economical to ask the beautiful Lady Di to meet the players at ground level.

BOUNCING

At some point on their procession, press photographers would force the team to line up for a souvenir group photograph, on which occasion they would 'bounce' on their haunches, now seizing the opportunity to sing their 'jaunty' Cup-final single, or else a rendition of our own beloved State Anthem, 'Here We Go Here We Go Here We Go Here We Go Here We Go Here We Go—oh'. Players would take turns in wearing the cup, its lid and its base as if they were hats, while the matchwinning goalscoring hero lounged on the turf in front of his oscillating team-mates, looking forward to the disappointment of the remainder of his career, and his subsequent employment as a 'celebrity' sales representative on the Wirral peninsula.

LOGIC COUNT: 9/10

During one short period of Western European history, 1945–85, male pattern baldness somehow ceased to be recognised as an indicator of prodigious testosterone production, personal charm and sexual invention. Therefore, it was quite logical at the time for the unrecognised harem leader to grow one side of his hair to fully 40 centimeteres in length and plaster disguising strands over his naked pate. One competing theory suggests that the flaunting of the supremely erotic 'spam-head' was deemed indecent, and players were ordered to cover their irresistible mating signal with their remaining hair, a hat, or any other suitable device at hand. Such as a recently gained football trophy.

THE TEAM BATH

When half the team had stripped naked and immersed themselves neck-deep in a large, water-filled hole in the dressing-room floor, their remaining colleagues took time out from swigging milk and ruining each other's television interviews to push their fully-clothed manager into this 'team bath'. Rather than mourning his ruined attire, he would join in celebrating its destruction by drinking apple wine from the cup, employed in this instance in its intended unhygienic purpose.

LOGIC COUNT: 2/10

Bathing was less efficient than showering because particles of dirt suspended in the water were able to realight on the body. The additional hazards of communal bathing include the transmission of germs and infection, prying television cameras, damp towel-flicking and Manchester City full-back Glyn Pardoe.

THE OPEN-TOP BUS

The victorious team, returning from their successful 'hunt' on an open-topped bus, milked plaudits from their adulatory 'tribe' (the people of their home city), echoing similar festive customs dating back to the age of cavemen, superimposed lizards and large furry bikinis.

LOGIC COUNT: 1,000,000 BC /10

'Ungowah!'

BREAKFAST IN BED

Two days after the Cup final, the lounging future sales representative would feature heavily on the reverse page of all smaller-format newspapers. Taking his final bow from the public arena, he would be pictured sitting in bed, reading an earlier newspaper story about how he came to claim his incidental place in football history. The player's 'landlady' would normally have balanced on his groin a) an invalid feeding tray, b) a high-carbohydrate breakfast meal, and c) a striped 'mug' of suffused tea leaves with excess sugar.

LOGIC COUNT: 950 calories/10

'He's a growing boy,' said a proud Mrs Butterworth.

73

FOOD IS TRENDY

A balanced, high-energy diet is vital for any sportsperson. That's why today's footballers all take a blue pill in the morning, and two speckly capsules at night. But SAMMY SPACE CADET has discovered a nostalgic alternative diet. Food.

Yo!?! In the fantastic olden days when there were dinosaurs, Labour governments and jokes about players smoking astroturf, cats and chicks used to eat this stuff called food. It was a bit like food pills, only it was bigger and it tasted of cake and gravy and bits of animals' bottoms!?!

Old-fashioned footballers ate food, so that makes it incredibly cool and fascinating, and I'm going to start a collection tomorrow. But for now I'm going to show you how to replicate your own foodie-style pre-match meal!?!

My in-depth research has already revealed that footballers ate slightly different diets to the ordinary people who weren't mega-trendy superstars: their active lifestyle demanded an intake of protein, vitamins and minerals which were not present in doner kebabs, the Western world's staple source of carbohydrates, congealed oil and chilli sauce.

Unlike the body of the population, the lean, mean, break-dancing machine that was a footballer's temple of skill received its bonus fix of chemicals from obscure substances known as 'ingredients'. And a more commonplace one called 'lager'!?!

THE PRE-MATCH SPREAD: GETTING IT RIGHT

Here is a typical pre-match 'spread', 'laid on' by a football digs landlady who really knew her stuff – packed full of essential ingredients and bite-sized fun for footballers.

Ingredients were monster kooky foodstuffs which could not be eaten until they had been mixed together and heated up. Ingredients had no pictures of squealing children on their packaging: they were bought in plain paper bags and boxes by old people and footballer's cooks, the only people who knew what to do with them. Look out for collectable footballing ingredients like flour, eggs, pearl barley and suet. Neato!?!

1. Bunch of Grapes
Note how the fruit has been sprinkled with the ace ingredient flour.

2. Cake
A source of many toppermost of the poppermost ingredients: flour, eggs, lard, cooking chocolate, almonds, gelatine flower decorations and flower petals (3 off).

3. Bread Sauce
Includes a) bread, b) milk, c) lard, and d) suet. Presented in gravy-boat at rear.

4. Water Biscuits
Ingredients include a) water, and b) biscuits.

5. Chocolates
Big up!?! Big up!?! Big up!?! for chocolate!?!

6. Peanuts
One bag off. Note: big peanuts were once known as 'cashews'.

7. Ice-cream with Fruit
The poor nutritional value of the fruit is balanced by a block of lemon Viennetta and a row of boiled sweeties.

8. Block of Lard
A fine and handsome ingredient.

9. Set of Dusters
For polishing cutlery and stuff.

10. Bunch of Flowers
Sprinkle cake with petals, as shown.

THE FOODIE-OMETER

See Matt Busby scanning George Best with the foodie-ometer in the 'All-Time Greatest-Ever Ireland XI' on pages 108–109!?!

The foodie-ometer was an electronic x-ray device commonly used in football's Golden Age. It enabled a coach to keep strict tags on the diet of his star charges, by indicating the nature and quantity of food intake currently passing through their digestive tract.

Matt Busby's featured examination of Best revealed he had egg and chips for tea, washed down with 17 pints of Worthington 'E'. For breakfast, he had a glass of Andrews' Liver Salts, a bowl of butterscotch-flavoured Ready Brek, a runny egg sandwich, two cups of tea and a bottle of Glenfiddich.

PRE-MATCH SPREAD: GETTING IT WRONG

1. Assorted Fruit
Fruit is useless because it does not contain ingredients to make it taste of chocolate or curry. Here are some bananas, apples and a tomato.
2. Bunch of Grapes
Note lack of healthy flour sprinkled on the fruit
3. Ice
Usually considered too cold to be a bona fide ingredient, ice does in fact constitute the boring half of ice-cream.
4. Glacé Cherries
Okay for starters, but where's the rest of the cake!?!
5. Orange Juice
Undisguised by the inclusion of cucumber segments, orange juice is still recognisable as the liquid from the middle of oranges. And oranges are only fruit.
6. Carnations
Nowhere near as groovy as the purple flowers in **Getting it Right**!?!
7. Nuts
And the same to you, matey!?!

DIET DURING MATCH: GETTING IT RON

Here are the famous football brothers Big Fat Ron and Not-So-Big Fat Graham Atkinson, pictured during their playing days at Oxford United. See how Graham gets on with the business of footy while 'hefty veteran' Ron loiters by the Popular Side refreshments stall, waiting for his mid-first-half pie.

YOU ARE WHAT YOU EAT
Every modern footballer should be an expert on meat, learning to distinguish whether pie ingredients originated from a sheep's bottom or a cow's bottom. Ideally, every modern footballer should know his ligaments from his tendons, his 8-track cartilages from his musicassettes and his big fat bottom from his elbow.

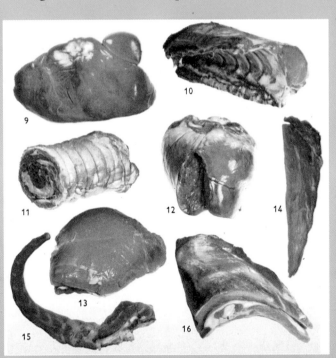

Digest and memorise: 9) liver; 10) loin (veal chops); 11) kidney roast (rolled); 12) torn cruciates (Paul Gascoigne); 13) nasty pulled hamstring; 14) nasty groin strain; 15) the baby monster who pops out of John Hurt's chest in *Alien*; 16) dislocated shoulder (Bryan Robson).

SPOT your ligaments . . .

EDISON SPEAK: A FOOT IN THE DOOR OF TIME

The Treasury's own door-stepping, time-travelling reporter beams back and forth through time to report live on pivotal moments in football's history . . .

Space Cadets, already they're calling this quite literally The Day That Football Died Of Shame. I'm speaking live from the Old Bailey, a big court in England. No one who endured this tawdry trial can help but feel soiled by the litany of grubbiness and greed to have unfolded these last few weeks, or rather unrolled, like a filthy old carpet, with fleas and stains and things hidden inside it. Things you wouldn't see when it was still all rolled up. While it was all still hidden. Like the truth.

I'm talking 2002, with its sordid new lexicon of shame: aqua-backhanders, bungs in buckets, cash-for-splash, and its conniving cartel of top tykes caught wet-handed by their selfish lusts for green lawns, luxury ponds and foamy baths on 'tap'.

During four gruelling weeks the jury heard how police painstakingly pieced together bits of the jigsaw, even though to start with all they had were loads of pieces that looked like the sky, and not a straight edge in sight. Nothing daunted, they gathered tiny morsels of evidence, speck by speck, until what lay before them were no longer supposition's dry crumbs, but a huge cake of truth, baked from fresh facts!

thank-yous for careless keeping, furtive hoses syphoned thousands of gallons of quite literally priceless aqua vita under the unseeing noses of the police.

From this court today go the guilty to their jails of shame. They include six whole boards and, amongst many others, Barnsley boss David Hirst, Leeds supremo Gary Pallister, Huddersfield's Chris Waddle and Sheffield United player-manager Brian Deane. Only Wednesday's David Pleat was

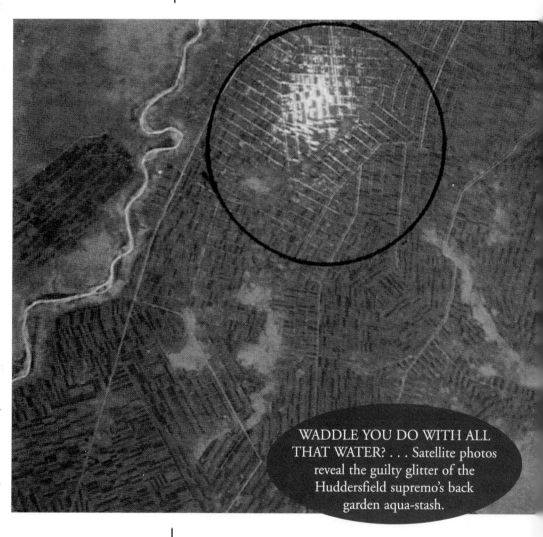

WADDLE YOU DO WITH ALL THAT WATER? . . . Satellite photos reveal the guilty glitter of the Huddersfield supremo's back garden aqua-stash.

The court heard of matches thrown by every Yorkshire team at some time between 1998 and 2001, thrown in return for late-night deliveries of water, sent north in tankers by shadowy southern syndicates known as the 'Rain Men'. At service stations in the parched fields of 'God's Country', barrels were loaded into sinister vans in return for missed penalties. A thirsty public was mocked as forged ration-books were swapped for loose marking at set-pieces and, as liquid

acquitted, convincing the jury that his team had genuinely tried to win all the games it lost.

Today we've seen a truly grubby thread woven into the rich warp and weft that is football's history. Your seat in the public gallery came courtesy of Edison Speak, putting my Foot in the Door of Time and reporting live for THE TREASURY.

BILLY McPHEE

Nobody calls me 'Freaky' McPhee any more. Not after what happened. It'd be nice to think that people just overcame their prejudice and decided not to be so shallow as to judge on appearance. It'd be nice. But it'd be wrong as well.

It was my parents who agreed to the research programme. They let me be pumped me full of untested drugs for the first ten years of my life; sold me to science in return for a house on the coast, an offshore account and sole rights to my story if it all went pear-shaped. Which, of course, it did.

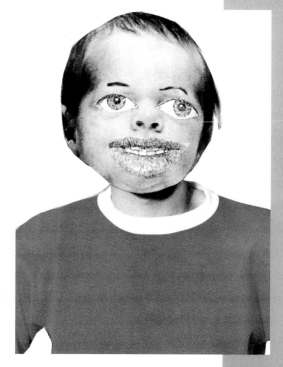

Or baby-shaped, to be precise. But I'm not here to talk about growth hormones, clones and smart-drugs gone stupid. I'm here to talk about football. What the drugs took from my face they gave to my feet. In other words, I'm as good at the game as I'm ugly.

Still, skill gets you nowhere if sponsors can't be found and posters don't sell. The kid with my face on her duvet cover is the kid who has nightmares. So despite my record (top scorer for school, youth and reserves), I never had a sniff of the first team. Word was I was only on the staff to keep up quotas, keep the Equal Ops red-tapers away.

That was before the game on Cazalin. Press expected a butchering and, to be fair, so did we. Especially when four went long-term sick with CJD. Boss tried loans, swaps, kids, the works. No luck. No choice either. He had to pick me, and I was ready. Cazalins gave me terrible stick, on and off the pitch, even before the game. (Bit rich really, given the state of some of them.) Even our travelling fans joined in. I put a stop though.

Never touched the ball till we were three down. But by the last ten, we were all square and I had a hat-trick. We had to win, a draw would be as bad as defeat. My timing was spot on. Last minute, I get the ball deep, go past three, run, dummy the shot, skin two more, do the keeper and . . . priceless. I'm on their goal-line, no one close. It's quiet, like the crowd's got one big, fat, stupid mouth, and the mouth is shut. All I can hear is the air-con whirring and our bench screaming: 'Bury it! Put it away!'

I rolled the ball slowly on to the line, half in, half out, just to be sure. Left it there and exited, stage left. Down the tunnel at a trot, as I recall, with noise levels rising a notch or three behind me. I didn't turn round. It felt more than sweet. The match had been mine; I'd saved it, won it, lost it. All of them, all down to one man, down to me: Freaky McPhee. I didn't catch the same shuttle home as the lads.

At the turn of the century, top sports counsellor Dr Irwin Sprinkler had unparalleled insight into the minds of sports stars. His book What it Takes: Sporting Success and Psychological Dysfunction was a worldwide bestseller, but professional ethics meant details of his private practice remained unpublished. Now THE TREASURY reveals previously unread reports, affording Space Cadets an unprecedented and surprising peep behind the curtain of sanity drawn across the windows of some 20th-century greats.

DR SPRINKLER'S CASEBOOK

ALAN SHEARER

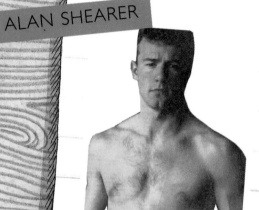

I damn near fell off of my chair when he called. Had him all figured for Mr Regular Guy: 'Chicken and beans, do my best for the football club, if I score it's a bonus, yadda yadda yah.' The whole schtick. Turns out the guy's walking a temperamental tightrope, but major league, like on dental floss across the Grand Canyon. The whole bit he does on TV; it's a front, a scam. This guy is wired! Crazy like a damn jackrabbit on speed. Says I gotta help on account of he's got this urge to take off and ride around Texas butt naked on a Harley with his friend Mr Daniels and, like, a whole carpet tile of lysergic. I had him in here and I gotta say, if I wasn't a respected psychologist with a Harvard doctorate, I'd say the guy's a total freaking Grade A psycho. The Mr Modesty routine's driving him nuts. Told me he loves Wagner and de Sade and French provincial cooking and paganism and rare first editions and that he always finishes the crossword before the little Le Saux guy but never says a word. The pressure he's under to act like a dork; says it's cooking his brain, says on a bad day he can actually hear it simmering in its juices. Begged me for Prozac. I gave him a yoga tape, breathing exercises and an appointment in a fortnight.

With Vinny, it's about three things: gender, gender and gender. Guy like that wears his masculinity on his sleeve. I tell ya, if testosterone could feed the starving, put Vinny in bottles and six months later you'd be selling 'em lo-cal potato chips. His problem is to access his feminine side. He's heard he should have one and, being the guy he is, he'd hate for anyone to find out, but he thinks it'd help him personally and professionally if he could locate what he calls his 'bird-space'. I have some panty-hose and fancy-schmancy robes in my office for just such occasions; we're going gently to start with and see if we can't have him go shop as a woman inside three months. Says he's already much more sensitive to the needs of his team-mates and more effective at set-pieces. Plus, last week he asked if he could use moisturising foundation AND a loose powder base on combination skin.

DAVID GINOLA

I know a professional oughta rise above it, but I gotta say, we all got favourites and this guy is mine. One: he has no problem talking about himself. Two: he's kinda well balanced already, compared to a lot of Brit footballers. Three: if he were any damn sexier I swear I'd grow a moustache, lift weights and wear my jeans kinda tight. Only reason he comes is the management up there figure he's got this Superiority Complex. David, I said, those guys are only half right. You don't have a complex but you are superior. You're better than them, deal with it! What a guy. I still have the crumpled Gauloises packet he tossed into my basket. He's French, by the way.

IAN WRIGHT

Don't know what else I can do for the guy. It's an identity thing. If he ain't angry, he just ain't Ian Wright, and if he ain't Ian Wright, he don't know who the damn hell he is, so he stays angry. I know one thing. I know he's got a huge beef with authority. Any authority. Referees, managers, traffic wardens, whatever. You got authority, Ian's your enemy. Plus he's got this whole respect thing going on. He was at some big store, the checkout girl, she says £43.78 or whatever the hell it cost and Ian just starts in on her about how she's giving him attitude and how she ain't showing him no respect and she'd better start looking for a new job and she's just a damn muppet. Couple a weeks ago I had him in here, made him dress up like a referee and really let him have it for half an hour. Like a role-play thing. Said he wanted to keep the shorts, on account of they felt kinda silky and nice on his legs. Told him he might have slightly missed the point and he tells me to get off his back and show some respect. By the time he left, I wanted to punch his damn lights out.

BARRY FRY

On the basis that mature, self-aware professionals sense their limitations, I gotta say quite openly that this little guy got me beat. I failed. Bombed, struck out, flopped, screwed up. He is nuts and science can not help him. There, I said it.

(Hey! You can't solve the puzzle if you haven't read the book!)

ACROSS

8. You give back endlessly before Revie, find where Nobby goes at night. (7)
9. Speedy's sexy suit's a hopelessly void globe. (9)
13. Unwise form of address on Planet Hard in Robson's Porto? (5)
14. Temporary transfer's confused about first gag, leads to half a trophy. (5)
15. The endless conflict with Lee Sharpe, initially (they've got horrible pointy nipple things). (7)
16. Is Big Eric's house also his cat water? (7)
17. Shaven heads take on shirts in the Inter-Ibiza Cup. (5)
18. Bruce goes to church on the Copacabana. (5)
20. How to avoid the taxman's tackle! (5)
22. Attention Zorro! He starred at the ColaDome in 2022. (6)
23. Oriental in troubled Ghanaian capital's a Brazilian. (6)
25. The facts at your fingertips! (8)

27. Allow one firm to follow a headless cat and Scarabula's Plutonians appear. (8)
30. Liz can work out where Freaky McPhee stunned the crowd. (6)
31. Make a turn after Alabama while Viv's around; scene of play-off fiasco. (6)
32. A chinwag establishes that Asprilla's are huge! (5)
35. Medic precedes something singular for Muska Muska's crowd noise. (5)
36. He's in front, seemingly in West Yorkshire. (5)
37. Light blow between two points makes everything go dark. (7)
39. Upset avatar admits a gram; ear muffs required here. (7)
41. Ruud in the first person? (1,3,1)
42. Frankly, there's no end to Sniffer. (5)
43. Cottoning on that the rebellion involves beer gone bad. (Turning a team into Madrid?) (9)
44. No smoking after the snap (they travel at the speed of light). (7)

CUNNING CRYPTIC CROSSWORD

DOWN

1. Dr Sprinkler's favourite is useless in goal. (6)
2. Where is it? Not in here, Scully. (3,5)
3. Soca job ruin! 2004 nap massacre victims (4,7)
4. Atkinson's hygiene problem in front of a statue for Strathclyde PanGlobal star. (9)
5. Accommodate trial to see who survives. (7)
6. Not as high amidst the great void, continentals play at this. (6,4)
7. They thought it all was. Then it was. (4)
10. Pearce loses love but finds direction. It's all in the mind. (6)
11. (and 21d) Maybe sage Goan adages reveal a time before sponsorship, space travel and synthetic fibres. (4,3,4,3)
12. Like half of that, mum, it makes breathing hard. (6)
19. Love writer in on gag's beginning sees a chance to score. (7)
21. See 11.

24. It's not the Left that follows walk out . . . but he's more fun to drink with than Shearer. (11)
26. Pinch barriers, like they did first at Old Trafford. (10)
28. Returning among sulphur and fumes, an unmarried maniac is disturbed, like the Galaphus Three. (9)
29. Coupling with pole, typical of a Heritage Ref! (7)
30. You and you, but without the room. (6)
32. Like pumas from Tokyo? (8)
33. Say, Ken! That's pretty underhand. (6)
34. As abject as a Red Star player? (7)
38. Pin fan dressed as 3S pioneer. (6)
40. In a reasonable game, where the crosses go. (4)

'CHEESE'

Top soccerologist DR SKORN translates the subconscious messages beaming out of history's team mugshots . . .

TINY ARSE

In actual size, this miniature portrait of an Arsenal team, a big wall and a clock showing 1.28 p.m. measured a mere 4 x 6 centimetres. It was given away free in a packet of sickly breakfast cereal. Not one of the players is identifiable. A clear case of endemic low self-esteem.

But wait. One microscopic player, seated second from left in the front row, has attempted to vent his personality. He has refused to follow two of the three time-honoured photographer's instructions to: a) fold your arms, b) look at the camera, and c) keep your knees together for reasons of decorum. It is the rebellious 'hippy' footballer Charlie George, hitting out in his own

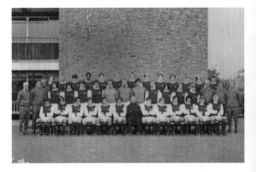

small way against the formality of the shot, and against its intended use as a capitalist bribe aimed at the youth of the day.

HOPEFUL GLAZIERS

Here is a Crystal Palace team-group in a 'triumphal' formation most typically adopted by the recent winners of a cup, or a trophy. Note that the object held aloft in celebratory fashion is neither a cup nor a trophy, but a football. It is to be assumed that the team were practicing the pose in anticipation of an occasion when it could be used in a more proper context. Records show they need not have bothered.

DISCOVATED PENSIONERS

The League Cup-winning Chelsea team of 1971–72 is captured here taking a well-earned rest outside their training-ground bar facility. The team is taking a break not from football training, but from drinking training. Alan Hudson and Charlie Cooke appear to be showing some signs of tiring, but the pair were well known for their 'second wind', and would doubtless, by midnight, be leading their team-mates' revelry on the stroboscopic discotheque dancefloors of London's King's Road.

MIGRATORY BLADES

Sheffield United adopt the flight formation of a gaggle of migrating Canada geese, giving out subconscious signals of graceful power, freedom with discipline and, hopefully, a 'high-flying' entry into Europe at the end of the season.

Sadly, United never lived up to the promise of their collective body-language. As shown in our photographic evidence, before the season had even started, skipper Eddie Colquhoun disastrously broke ranks to fill in that big hole in the Bramall Lane pitch.

ESPAÑA 82

CHILE

ALIEN INVASION ALERT! ALIEN INVASION ALERT!

Spot the two 'small grey' aliens playfully infiltrating this Chilean group shot from the 1982 World Cup. Of course this race of keen time-tourists is invisible to the naked eye, with evidence of their holidaymaking only appearing retrospectively on film.

PROUD CHERRIES

Earthlings claim it is possible, more than a century on, to sense a certain revolutionary pride emanating from this much sought-after Bournemouth souvenir picture; but all too often it proves impossible for an illogical mind to separate football facts from their context. And everybody knows the tragic Bournemouth story.

Objectively, only the team's manfully clenched stomach muscles may symbolise a strength of will in defiance of authority (the podgy member fourth in the row was, incidentally, no turncoat: he simply did not hear the photographer shout 'suck').

For this was the Bournemouth side which stood together in revolt against a distasteful close-season kit-change. Their new shiny crimson and pink jerseys (with gull-wing tie-up collars, Adidas epaulettes, and a large central Pop Art cherry badge) were rejected as 'too poofy'. The team bravely opted to play out their league programme as 'skins'. And the freezing winter of 1972 took its terrible toll . . .

CONFUSED STAGS

In an attempt to go one better than their local rivals from Sheffield, Mansfield Town's first-team squad fared even worse with this ill-conceived migratory pattern. The Stags ended up not flying south into Europe, but instead trotting backwards into the Fourth Division.

GLODSHEDDLL

ALiENBAWL

LX FRRGASSIANN

LIFE IN THE DUG-OUT:
A VIEW FROM THE GAFFAPOD

You might think being a manager these days means being on intimate terms with insanity, but the plight of today's bosses is a slab of space-cake compared with what their predecessors used to endure. We downloaded our data to 'Big' Bob Batch/Elor, the modern game's most 'colourful' boss. And, exclusive to THE TREASURY, here's what he made of his job description all those years ago.

DAY TO DAY

I'll be straight with you. Couldn't have handled it. I've had a butchers at the data, and I can't see how they've done it. First up, they've to be with just the one club, which is basically a bit of an eggs-and-basket thing from the off. Plus they've to turn up every day, actually at this one club, get their lads to run about in circles, buy and sell players, talk to media folk, plan tactics, the works. I don't get it. I mean, I do okay, me portfolio's up to seven teams at the minute, though me broker'd rather it were ten, and even though one of 'em's on Outer Travilisc, I still only work mornings, other than match days. This lot, most of 'em spend half the time in and out the shower, tracksuits, muddy boots and what-not. Can't remember when I were last in a changing-room, which is just as it should be, as it goes. Having your team see you change, it's derogative to morale and good order. Take it from me, one sniff of the boss's knackers and respect's down the SaniFlo fast as you can say prickly heat.

MATCH DAY

I don't get it, not at all. Apart from an ulcer, a sore throat and perhaps a right-hander from an angry fan, what's to be gained from spending the match jumping about in that daft little hutch with no door on? What'll happen is, you'll spend all day screaming at your left-back to stick one up the winger, and cos he can't hear or he's too fat and slow, you'll waste all of a time-out telling him what a useless arse he is. Pointless. Compare that with what I get done in me GaffaPod. I've a ten-camera link up, slo-mo on request, two assistants constantly sifting and feeding me MatchStats and I'm live to the changing-rooms. So I've got their full attention before, during and after, and if someone's dropped a bollock there's no argument cos I can just show 'em the replay. And if I do need to gee 'em up a bit, I can always have me coach Billy sling the cups about and what-have-you.

CONDITIONS OF EMPLOYMENT

Far as I can make out there used to be this 'loyalty' thing, which I suppose was fair enough if you were meant to be managing just the one team at a time, but it didn't last. There was the McGhee Protocol for one thing, in '98 or '99, and after that it looks like you could do pretty much what you liked. Swings and roundabouts, really. I mean, just now I'd be hard pushed to remember off the top of me head the names of all the players in me teams, and I don't suppose many got away with that in those days, but they were harder to sack then. It's all me contracts, it's industry-standard, lose x number

NᴼᴼM ★ NɪYN

SɪR BARRY FRY

MANAGËRS
NᴼᴼM ★ OₒN3

VV

VEYKIN - VEEGKAN

MANAGËRS
NᴼᴼM ★ OₒNA

BEEGFAH - TRONN

of games or fail to win y number of cups and that's it, binned off, down the road, Bob. Back then, if your best mate was the club chairman or you knew who he was shagging or what he was skimming off the top, you were made. Bosses then used to whine about insecurity and iffy boards and that, but out of all me clubs I've only ever met one owner, and that was by chance in a dodgy VR-Bar on Venus.

THE PLAYERS

No comparison, really, is there? I mean, back then, your boss was like your dad, teacher, probation officer and spiritual guru as such. For meself, I'm not sure why any normal grown-up would want to spend so much time with a bunch of soft lads. From what I can make out, you'd not just turn up at away games, you'd actually have to travel on the same vehicle with them! What's that all about then? Three days on a Shuttle with any of my lot, all betting on horses, throwing their food about, doing SimuSex and lighting farts, that'd be me out the game for good. Bosses then, they'd always say as how they enjoyed being with their lads and getting to know them in so many words. Now I'm sorry, but I were brought up to believe that your family's for enjoying and getting to know and your players are for instructing in tactics, technique, positional sense and such. Confuse them two conscripts and you're staring up the barrel of smelling the starch on the white coats and getting your bumps felt.

JOB SATISFACTION

I'm not convinced as how it applied. Even if you won something once in a while, there'd still be someone spitting on your motor car, posting dog waste to your grandmother or making stuff up in the 'newspapers' about how you like the old fella wedged up a loose lady now and again. Granted, some of them – your Barmbies, McAllisters, Dublins and that – they've had a nice life, fancy cars, plenty 'money' and so forth; but I always thought pressure was going out on pens to Proxima Falafel. Put me under half that pressure and I reckon I'd just burst like a big fat bluebottle caught in a time compression. No stomach for it, you see.

MANAGËRS
NᴼᴼM ★ AYT7

L ★ VENËRABL

MANAGËRS
NᴼᴼM ★ TWON

PBLEËAT

MANAGËRS
NᴼᴼM ★ TRE8

KLUᵤF-E

AN AUDIENCE WITH THE IMMORTAL GORDON

'Immortal', like 'tragic' or 'lovely', is one of those superlatives bandied about all too frequently. The fabulous world of football is as guilty as anyone of such hyperbole. But THE TREASURY is proud to present an exclusive interview with a man fully deserving of the title 'Immortal', because, well, that's exactly what he is! Gordon Strachan looks about 55, but was born 140 years ago in 'Edinburgh'. Though he rarely speaks to the press these days, he agreed to talk to us about his life and times and the last hundred years or so.

Firstly, Immortal, please accept our thanks for agreeing to this interview.
Just call me Gordon, please. And it's a pleasure, really.

Perhaps you could begin by telling our readers how you feel?
Just great, thanks. I've had a nasty wee cold, mind, and this ear infection with a load of leaky, gunky stuff, but generally I'm great, yeah.

Do you keep up with the game?
Oh yeah, definitely. Let's face it, I've nothing much else. My family's mostly dead. I've a few great grandkids, but we've not much in common. Bairns these days are a wee bit wild for my liking, and anyway, how are they supposed to know who I am? So, yeah, football. I'm pretty much a seven-days-a-week man.

Any team in particular? Or players?
Well, obviously, you can't ignore Venus at the minute, they're on a tremendous run. They look unstoppable, and I'd say their front three's as attractive an attacking line-up as I've seen in years.

How do they compare with the greats from your day?
Och, well, it's a different game, isn't it? I mean, these young Venusians are fine players all right, don't get me wrong. But there used to be more skill in the game. Players had more technique and it was slower, you could put your foot on the ball and look around. Nowadays, players are so fit it's all crash-bang-wallop, warp-factor 4 stuff. You don't get the artistry.

You must tire of the question, Gordon, but do you or the doctors have any idea how you've come to stay alive?
Well, I've certainly got no idea, and if the doctors have, they've never let me in on it. It's a long time ago now, but as far as I can remember, I got to about 60, and that was just sort of it. The prostate, the arthritis, memory loss, organ failures, all of that, nothing. Just a wee bit of sciatica from my playing days. But then 50 years or so ago they figured out spine transplants, so I've got the backbone of a 40-year-old now.

No special secrets for all your Space Cadet fans, then?
I'm afraid not, Space Cadets, just plug in the Vit-Drip twice a week like mum says, and wear your vest all year round.

Perhaps this isn't really a fair question, Gordon, but looking back at your career now, are there any regrets?
(Pauses, sighs) Well, I don't know. Maybe. I'm not a great one for regrets, really, but I'd have to say now - and it's very easy with hindsight, obviously - that going to Coventry wasn't perhaps the best bit of business I ever did.

I'm sorry, 'Corventry'?
Yeah, in '95, when I left Leeds.

I'm sorry, 'Corventry' doesn't ring a bell at all.
Coventry, no, you'll not find much mention of them now and, well, it wasn't the happiest time. I was keen to get on, and I thought it'd happen quicker there than at Leeds, so I left.

But - forgive me, its a long time ago, it's history to me - you did end up back at Leeds, didn't you?

Oh yeah, in the end I did, but that was later on, during all the mergers and big deals and what-not. Leeds had to merge with Bradford and Huddersfield and become the West Yorkshire Warriors. Slippery slope, really. Then the Sheffield teams got involved, and eventually you just had this huge North of England thing, with Man U and Newcastle and Liverpool as well, and, you know, for a while it was just havoc and -

Hmm, yes, that's really interesting, Gordon, thanks. I wonder, though, could we talk about you again? If you could have looked ahead all those years ago and seen what the world's like now, what would have surprised you most, do you think?

Apart from the price of a pint of milk?

Apart from that, yes.

Well, for one thing, all the business about galaxies and milky ways and solar systems. That was all just books and films in those days. Little green men and folk wrapped in tinfoil and all that. We thought putting a flag on the moon, taking a year to send a wee camera up to Mars, we thought that was pretty smart and about as far as we'd get. I mean, it was hard enough playing against Brazilians. If you'd said we'd be playing Venusians as well, we'd probably have thought you were taking the piss.

So it's safe to say things are a bit different now then?

You could say that, yeah. I think the biggest difference is with countries and rivalries like that. I mean, 100 years or so ago, I was dead into the idea of 'Scotland', y'know? I played for them 50 times and I was so proud of it. England were, y'know, the enemy. Your flag, your shirt, all that, it was just the most important thing, you can't imagine what it was like, but now it's like, 'What is Scotland?' I mean even me, now, with all my caps, I couldn't tell you where the border with 'England' used to be.

And does that make you sad?

No, not at all, I think it's great. It's so much less hassle for one thing. Now we're all sort of together and we just hate those Martian bastards!

And I suppose knowing you were immortal all those years ago might have made a difference as well.

Too bloody right it would! Fags, beer, cake, scotch, pizza; I never touched the stuff. Lived like a hyperactive bloody monk. Extra training, early nights, natural bloody spring water, seaweed tablets, all that. Christ, if I'd known then, I'd have made the boy Gascoigne look like the Virgin bloody Mary. I tell you, I'd have given that young Gary Speed a run for his money as well, you know. Always reckoned himself the ladies' man, did young Gary, but I'm telling you, they used to pay me more than a little attention as well, you know, yes, they did actually, red hair or no red hair, but oh no, not me, I was Gordon Strachan, family man, professional athlete . . .

SAMMY SPACE CADET got Striker and Wembley and the Space-uteo referee and linesman set for his birthday, so ner.

Football games from the past are really mega and tabletopocious. They make modern games look like the dog's bollocks because they are so obscure and ethnic. Who needs games like Klone-Your-Own fantasy football when you've got authentic tiddly-wink superstars!?! Who wants to create their ideal player from cloned body-parts and send him to play in galactic Virtual Reality leagues when you've got a dice, a scorepad and a 100-year-old drinking-straw!?! Eh???

Blow by Blow

BLOW FOOTBALL is a really mega DIY game dating from football's Dark Ages, when Liverpool used to win everything every year!?! It involves two straws, a ping-pong ball and pints of drool expended all over the pitch/moon-dome carpet in pursuit of satisfaction. If you play for long enough it is almost as groovy as doing an Airfix kit without ensuring there is adequate ventilation. You get the same kind of swirly headache as when you sit up dead close to the videoscreen. And everybody knows that's Coolsville Central Station!?!

Inaction Man

Imagine the frustrations of being my fab original ACTION MAN FOOTBALLER!?! You've got hands that can shoot a rifle, but you can't pick up your half-time cuppa. You keep getting toynapped by my sister, and forced to play doctors and nurses with Sindy. You can't stand on one leg without a custom-made prop; and even then you can only pose, not kick. You're deep in John Barnes territory, matey!?! You've even got the same bionic elastic cartilage in your gammy antique knees!?!

Mutant Striker

It wasn't just those Subbuteo players who refused to get down off their wobbly circus podiums – miniature football history is jam-packed with crazy hipsters and space mutants!?! WADDINGTON'S TABLE FOOTBALL stars were all born with a large plastic tiddly-disc instead of feet; STRIKER players had their nervous systems rewired so their leg shot up when you hit them on the head . . . and in BOBBY CHARLTON'S CASDON SOCCER, two control knobs operated Venusian teams that swivelled round to boot a marble with their ice-hockey stick legs!?!

Squelch!?!

Millions of years ago, every time you bought a cheap plastic football toy, they gave your dad four gallons of petrol for free!?! The offer covered all kinds of cosmically collectable player busts (!?!), coins, club badges, snazzy beakers in plastic holders, and SQUELCHERS – little booklets full of fascinating footy facts, so cool and trendy it wasn't just space-kids who collected and played SQUELCH! with them. The idea was for grown-ups to use their free petrol to take them to the pub and argue!?!

When I am old enough to blast off on alcohol pills, it will be my ambition to stride into The Gazza and GameBoy and hear some unhip bar-bore say something like, 'All a great goalkeeper needs on a rainy day are his cap and gloves.'

'SQUELCH!?!' I shall then reply, referring to my portable plastic wallet database. 'Zamora of Spain was never without his broom, which he used to keep his goalmouth tidy. He hated mud and dirt.' Or if the bar-bore said, 'No footballer is allowed to smoke on the field of play,' then I would SQUELCH!?! him with 'During a Scottish Cup-tie, Arbroath beat Bon Accord 36–0 while the Arbroath goalkeeper smoked his pipe under an umbrella throughout the game.' And I could go on . . .

Board Games

WEMBLEY and SOCCERAMA, with their dice, their square of cardboard and tiny plastic players, were exceptionally realistic football games. They worked on the groovily simple principle that money bought expensive players, which in turn brought success. Unless your team was Blackburn Rovers!?!

GOLDARN GROWN-UPS hi-jack Binky Banks' Subbuteo, Xmas 1968

Subbuteo Space Cadet Test

SUBBUTEO is skill, and I am Space Cadet champ of the solar system. I will take on all-comers provided we play at my house and I get to be Rotherham United. You've got to flick to kick properly, and no whacking the goalposts across the floor with your goalie rod. But first, you've got to take my test and answer yes to every question to prove you are a real Space Cadet and a worthy opponent.

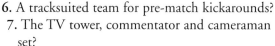

Do you, or have you ever owned:

1. A grandstand with floodlights so you can play in the dark?
2. Any figurines customised with number stickers – or paint, to resemble individual players?
3. A logbook of match results in your imaginary Subbuteo League?
4. The official scoreboard with alphabet 'for all the half-time scores'?
5. The subs' bench, manager and 'famous England mascot' set?
6. A tracksuited team for pre-match kickarounds?
7. The TV tower, commentator and cameraman set?
8. St John's ambulancemen, patient and policemen set?
9. A set of posts for official practice dribbling?
10. The official Subbuteo club flagpole?

See you on Tuesday night when my mum is out at popmobility!?! We can play under floodlights!?! Bring your own 'corner-kicker' ball-raising device!?!

FOURTH-ROUND HIGHLIGHTS
FOOTBALL UNIVERSE CUP 2097

MIGHTY MORPHIN POWER RANGERS 0
MYSTERONS 2

Right from the start, the twin 0–0 torch-beams on the stadium wall spelled out how the Martians intended to play this one. But the invisible spoilers had no answer to the Superhoops' superior movement off the ball: mainly flying kung-fu kicks and bouncing through the air on trampolines after just-pretend explosions . . .

THE CLANGERS 0
SPECTRUM 9

This afternoon the Spectrum lads put all their internal club problems behind them to score an emphatic Cup victory over knitted opposition. An initial dressing-room dispute centred on the question of captaincy – it turns out all the Spectrum lads are used to being captain! And then came a heated disagreement over which away kit most needed a boost in replica sales – with scarlet, blue, green, ochre, black and cynical blue-and-white stripes all receiving one vote each.

Captain Scarlet was finally accepted as skipper because he is indestructible, and each of the other captains went ahead and wore their own colour away kit, with little danger of being mistaken for a Clanger.

A miserable day for the Soup Dragon in the Clanger goals was completed when a sudden downpour rusted him to the spot and waterlogged his woollen back line. At that point, even the promising Under-21 Tiny Clanger's head dropped, along with the pitch of the loveable space-rodents' whistles.

For Spectrum, the Angels – Destiny, Harmony and Symphony – were a revelation on the wing, and Captain Ochre came off the minor characters' bench to impress with a second-half hat-trick. It was really great, how this little microphone popped down out of his cap . . .

THE TREASURY'S GUIDE TO PLANET REF

ONE: THE XALON

PROFILE:

On Xalon, the actual playing of football is forbidden by statute. Adult Xalons are bred only to officiate, and so regard themselves as the absolute pinnacle of reffing excellence. The first ref-race to arm itself, Xalons brook no interference from outside agencies, whether organic or chip-based. Use of AutoScan and MicroVision is scorned, as is the practice of easing on-field tensions with a laugh and a smile. Xalons never play advantage.

STRENGTHS:

A match reffed by a Xalon will not suffer from dissent, niggly fouls, mass brawls, tiresome stoppages or time-wasting. You've never seen a wall retreat 10 metres so fast.

WEAKNESSES:

A match reffed by a Xalon is unlikely to end with a full complement of players on each side. Dismissals are only marginally more frequent than summary dismemberings.

TYPICAL XALON RESPONSE TO A LATE, HIGH TACKLE:

'Come over here, number six. You're the disease, sonny, and I'm the cure.'

MOST FAMOUS XALON:

Lazlo the LawBringer, whose execution of Paul Ince in his testimonial for Manchester City in 2010 is still a top-selling screensaver almost 90 years on.

TWO: THE SAGACIAN

PROFILE:

The wisest of all refs, Sagacians officiate only in groups of three ('colloquia') and only when their combined ages exceed 200 years. ('Verily, for wisdom is as a fruit whose flesh grows sweeter with the years', Sagacian motto.) To counteract the disadvantages of old age, they maximise the virtues of positioning and anticipation and reach decisions by voting. They referee unarmed, but, on occasion, can be hurtfully critical.

STRENGTHS:

Fiercely impartial. No decision is reached without rigorous intellectual scrutiny. Rare is the Sagacian-reffed game that ends without most players having acquired a freshly-minted maxim.

WEAKNESSES:

Rigorous intellectual scrutiny can mean games delayed for hours while they debate moral absolutism with reference to intentional handball. Old age means numerous interruptions for toilet-breaks

TYPICAL SAGACIAN RESPONSE TO A LATE, HIGH TACKLE:

'Which of us truly denies that beneath the breast beats a second, savage heart, equally bent on evil? You're booked, number six.'

MOST FAMOUS SAGACIANS:

The Galaphus Three, whose famous 'onside, but morally offside' verdict was described in *The Sun* as 'the best bit of wisdom since Solomon offered to slice up the baby'.

The last 100 years have seen a bewildering array of refs taking charge of games galaxy-wide. But who were they? Where did they come from? Were they any good? The Treasury looks at the men and machines in the middle who've made the most waves down the years.

GOLDARN 4th OFFICIAL! Never misses a trick . . .

THREE: THE OMNIREF (™)

PROFILE:
An attempt to harmonise pan-Galactic standards of refereeing, the OmniRef is a state-of-the-art, 22nd century solution to a long-term design problem. The size of a cooking apple, the weight of a pencil and the consistency of chewing gum, the OmniRef hovers at heights of its own choosing, flies at the speed of sound, and registers input from invisible antennae spanning 360 degrees (eyes in the back of its head). Fluent in every known language.

STRENGTHS:
The OmniRef is incapable of a 'wrong' decision, as it can record, replay on a giant screen, zoom in and adjudicate on any action taking place within a 5km radius inside 0.0061 seconds.

WEAKNESSES:
Killing the game as a spectacle; no more dissent, anger, excuses or Joe Kinnear. Can't strike up humorous 'rapport' with players. Filling shorts with tin-foil can render players invisible to it.

TYPICAL OMNIREF RESPONSE TO A LATE, HIGH TACKLE:
'Level: 17.376cm too high: Timing: 1.438 seconds late. You're booked, number six. Watch yourself, or you're off. Message ends.'

MOST FAMOUS OMNIREF:
Alpha4T (cx/U7), the third ever made and the only one to malfunction. Due to chip-glitch, it endlessly replayed on the giant screen a couple making love in a house 4km away.

FOUR: THE 20TH-CENTURY 'HERITAGE REF'

PROFILE:
Heritage Refs (HRs) are currently popular due to the 20th-century nostalgia boom. Advances in cloning have made possible the creation of bespoke refs; 2096's most popular names were Malcolm, Paul and David, and most users opted either for the 'teacher from Arbroath' or 'freight manager from Chorley' model. In a sterile, chip-driven age, HRs are seen as glorious throwbacks to a golden age of inconsistency, fussiness and excess body-fat.

STRENGTHS:
Unafraid to trust their judgement and make snap decisions in heated atmospheres, the most in-demand models have a range of amusing tics and postures with which to delight and entertain crowds.

WEAKNESSES:
Flip-side of the above: inconsistent, self-important, oblivious to reason and unwilling to accept blame. Happiest when he's the game's main talking point. Looks a state in a tight shiny shirt.

TYPICAL HR RESPONSE TO A LATE, HIGH TACKLE:
Not applicable, didn't spot it. He was telling the midfield maverick to tuck his shirt in when it happened.

MOST FAMOUS HR:
Malcolm Dodds, a PE teacher from Arbroath cloned to ref the 2068 Galactic Series, was sonically unfleshed by angry Grudons after failing to spot Trion's use of anti-matter to protect their goal.

FAN-TASTIC FOOTY PICTURE QUIZ

Calling all telepathic readers!?! Pit your minds against the rockingly retentive retro recall of me, SAMMY SPACE CADET!?!

FBI ALIEN GO-GO BLACKMAIL ALERT!

1. Correct. The belly-dancer has now succeeded in attracting the attention of Netherland's brilliant footballer and 'problem boy' Johann Cruyff.

2. Correct. Answer unprintable in **SPACE CADETS' TREASURY**.

ODD MAN OUT

3. Correct. Paul Atkinson (Watford) is the odd man out because he was never a total flop as a manager.

4. Correct. Peter Shilton (Leicester) is the odd man out because he is wearing earmuffs and a cheesy grin, but no ill-judged 'fighter-pilot' tash.

5. Correct. Peter Shilton's moustache was expunged from Earth history in 1982. Totting-ham fans just wish Osvaldo Ardiles had been, too.

ACTING THE GIDDY GOAT

6. Correct. These footballers from the Dawn of Time are acting the giddy goat.

7. Correct. During the pre-match kickaround, they are lulling the opposition into a false sense of security by a) practising throw-ins; b) balancing in stupid positions; c) hurling abuse; d) wiping mud off the ball, and d) hovering in mid-air. (Score 1 point each.)

8. Correct. Straight from kick-off, they charge the unprepared enemy camp and notch a beauty. One-nil, old boy!?!

PLANET STARTERFORTEN

9. Correct. This action shot of Alan Hansen bringing down Everton full-back David 'Rhino' Unsworth was taken on Planet Nickname.
10. Correct. Planet Perspective is a planet where there is no perspective.
11. Correct. During his playing days on Planet Nickname, Planet Perspective President Jimmy Hill was known as 'The Rabbi'!?!

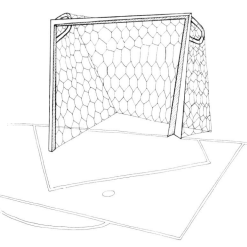

21 © 1967 A.T.V OVERSEAS LTD

CAPTAIN SCARLET AND THE MYSTERONS

ANGLO CONFECTIONERY LTD

FACE IN THE CROWD

15. Correct. Millwall Athletic versus Bolton Wanderers, Football League Division 2, 14 February, 1970.
16. Correct. The space alien in the goldfish-bowl helmet is thinking, 'Six light years round trip to watch this blinkin' rubbish.'
17. Correct. The human spectator in the centre of the picture is thinking about a scene involving stockings, satsumas, a short length of rubber hosing and his most excellent raincoat.

SPACE FAMILY CLOUGH

12. Correct. This is a picture of Derby County manager Brian Clough pulling up the big plastic pants of his daughter, Nigel Clough's sister.
13. Correct. Nigel Clough is the prematurely attitude-ridden Junior Space Cadet on the right.
14. Correct. Nigel may well, in fact, be the attitude-ridden Junior Space Cadet on the left.

Yo!?! How did *you* do, Mindreading Quiz Fan Dude???
Score 18–21: You already know how you did!?!
Score 15–17: You scored maximum points!?!
Score 11–14: With 75 most excellent bonus points thrown in
Score less than 11: for not letting on to all the other Space Cadets how I secretly sent off for that scientifically-proven irresistible hormone spray with its glossily illustrated instruction leaflet entitled *How to Attract Girls and Stop the Big Boys With Underarm Hair from Space Academy Kicking Moondust in Your Face*. Oh, drat.

PLAYING AWAY:
THE VOICE OF THE FANS

Most of us prefer to watch the big game on VidSpex™ from the comfort of a DigiPad™, but there have always been fans long-suffering enough to follow their teams and support them wherever they play. These determined Nostalgists have been printing their own underground records ('fanzines') since the 20th century, and from such rich sources we reproduce a few brief accounts of the perils they've faced, year in, year out.

FOOD

'Trans-Matter Migrators always do your guts in good style, but we was still well up for nosebag before the game. Billy's give us earache all the way there about Saturn meat and how it's always cat or space-monkey, but he's still legged it to the first dodgy-looking snack-shack, slapped down his GrubSwipe and gone for the Saturn Special Three-Meat Sundae. For his ten debits he gets this, I dunno, this thing, like a big-nosed rat in a teacake. Three mouthfuls in, there's this horrible squeaking noise, Billy's honking his guts into the gutter and his Three-Meat Sundae's shot away up an air-con duct with its arse hanging off. Me and the boys, we've creased, lost it. Billy says next time we take the Migrator he's bringing corn-beef sandwiches. No one's had the heart to tell him dead flesh ages a month each minute it's inside the Migrator. He'll find out for himself, but we'll all be well gone when he opens his lunchbox.'

(From *My Old Man's A Spaceman: EurAsia FC on Tour, 2042-43*)

THE WEATHER

'If Eltran's got a wetter moon than Haxilon I've yet to see it. You don't get drizzle or showers or squalls on Haxilon, just rain. In their brief summers, there's a one in ten chance of a nice space-fog; the excitement bring Haxiles on to the walkways in their tens. But mainly it rains and they stay in. Trevor's Space-Cart was in for new boosters; Jem said no bother, we could take the Arrow. We mentioned that Alpha Valuvi play-off fiasco. He said no problem, he'd had the thrusters re-grooved. We said okay. Three weeks it took us, and he's that tight he hadn't paid his TV subs, so the only channel we had was the free one, Weather Channel. If we'd had Football Channel we might have heard on the way that the game was off. Water-logged pitch. Jem knew a short-cut home, bypassing the bottleneck at Klarg. Took us a month. When we got home, Barry had been sacked, Paul's wife had left him, it was raining and we'd missed the cup draw. It's Haxilon. Away.'

(From *Astral Weeks: A Year in the Life of Pacific FC, 2037*)

GETTING IN

'Alan blames Man U for SwipeWalls, but his grandad was a Leeds fan. Still, you can see his point. The Edwards-Fence, as introduced at Old Trafford in 2006, predated the SwipeWall. But not even Martin Edwards can have imagined his simple admission credit-test would turn out like those on Leftika C. We worked out you must have to be on at least Euro-70K to get in to the LeftikaDome. I'd paid my gas, 'leccy and eco bills the week before, and cleared half the year's Earth-Charge, but my card still flashed red because I didn't have enough Rupes in the Dishbank. Bob was bleeped early because he doesn't pay the Clean-Air Levy by direct debit and Alan didn't even get to whip out his SwipeCard; his wrist barcode showed unpaid parking fines in his family going back 40 years. Oddly, it also revealed his grandad was a Leeds fan. Unless we as fans do something soon, the game's going to be out of reach for all but the super-rich before 2100.'

(From: *Solar So Good!* general fanzine, 2045)

TOILETS

'Memo to any Space Cadets thinking of travelling to see their team on Vargon: fast for a week or take plenty SaniSacs™. Our trip to Athletico Vargon FC revealed Personal Waste Facilities of truly 20th-century squalor. The PR-Mail mentioned a "gleaming shrine to ultra-hygiene", but we might almost have been at "Newcastle" in 1988! The hour or so we spent pre-match on a most agreeable Alco-Drip (can't fault the Vargonese space-grape!) under-standably left us in need of some outflow management. Ushered by typically surly Vargonese stewards towards the PWFs, imagine our horror to find: i) "cubicles" where a flesh/plastic interface was un-avoidable; ii) "urinals", where our own untreated liquid waste visibly flowed within centimetres of our shoes, and iii) surely the only sheets of "toilet tissue" to survive outside of a Heritage Dome. Pan-Universal Love's fine by the Mid-Earth Crew, but if a Vargonese offers you the tentacle of friendship, make sure you're wearing a space-mitt before shaking. You can't be too careful.'
(From *No one Likes Us, and That Hurts*, AFC Mid-Earth, 2061)

TROUBLE

'Ever been gobbed on by a Thwarl? It stings, and you'll have bumps as big as a spacedog's bollocks if you don't get it washed. We hate Thwarl. Ever since they spawned us out the Inter-Solar on pens. Tried to run us after, but we *stood!* and it

shit 'em right up. Thwarls got no legs so they look right soft tarts when they run. A few marbles or mint imperials under their castors and they've had it. Question: How many Thwarls does it take to change a lightbulb? Answer: None, they don't need 'em 'cos they think the sun shines out of their arses! Last time, right, we've had no protection off the Thwarl Bill. Met us off the shuttle and just let us loose in town. Which is basically just asking for it. Specially with their lot going round like they own the place. Lozza's still got the scars, got cornered by a bunch of them and they kept stinging him with those horrible pointy nipple things. Still, you've gotta laugh. Alec's turned round and said, "Oi, you must feel a right tit!" We cracked up. Right tit! Geddit?'
(From *Two World Wars and One World Cup*, Chelsea FC, 2032)

Speak like the Stars

Space Cadets – sign up now for a fan–tastic football nostalgia language course. Simply touch the authentic original star message you would like to deliver. Listen to the futuristic miniaturised computer recording, and repeat. Drop casually into conversation – wow chums and chumettes with your amazing antiquated soccer slang.

No. 4:

Speak like a Scouser, soft lad . . .

Greeting a Chum with Robbie Fowler

Phrase: 'R. A. R. kid. Sound shell-suit, like. Dey do do dat dere doh don't dey? Come 'ed soft kex.'
Translation: 'Hello.'

Warning to Razor: 'How tickled I ham, Doddy's diddy Diddymen. Nick-nacky nick-nack nicky-nacky-noo.'
Translation: 'Watch the boy Cottee ghosting in on the back stick.'
Note: All Liverpudlians were 'natural comedians'. Achieve the textbook delivery of this vintage Fowlerism with the use of a 'tickling stick' – an amusing comedy duster once brandished by all fun-loving Scousers.

Talking TV with Steve McManaman

Use this handy and versatile phrase to discuss plot development in a televisual soap-opera which went off air 76 years ago:
'Dere's notton down for dat Barry Grant. Minty shell-suit, like. Jimmy Corkhill's give 'im down de banks.'

Even in modern-day Space-Base Fab 4, add spice to any football conversation with the following time-honoured Steve-style observation:
'A, yer big blue soft-ollie, Everton are nowt burraloada woollybacks.'

Getting Interviewed with Ian Rush

Although Ian Rush was not technically a Liverpudlian, taking the piss out of his accent is nevertheless irresistible at this point:
Response to any question:
'Wellairmasawmechancelike knowharrameanlike adjustititfairsttime airknowhorrameanlikeair cheersbarry.'
Meaning: None.
Hint: For added authenticity of delivery, surgically remove Adam's apple and replace with average-size satsuma.

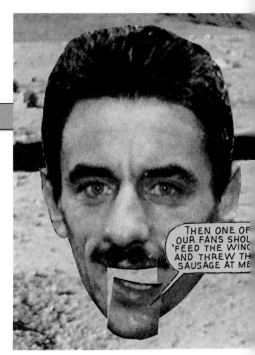

THEN ONE OF OUR FANS SHO[U]L[D] 'FEED THE WIN[G] AND THREW TH[E] SAUSAGE AT ME

SCUM! SCUM! SCUM!

THREE: HULL CITY v HARTLEPOOL UNITED

Hartlepool and Hull? Really?
Yep. One of the late 20th century's fiercest rivalries.

Why?
Proximity, mainly. Hull was just ten miles or so up the north-east coast of England from Hartlepool. Both towns were industrial and football-mad.

And they each had their own special identity, did they?
Not half! Hull: black and white, noisy, brash, 'funny', fanatical. Hartlepool: red and white, more cynical, less successful, latterly poorer, but once the so-called 'Bank of England' club, also fanatical (the 'Roker Roar').

NOT BIG, NOT CLEVER . . . Silly Hull fans push and shove

Nothing to do with 'religion' then?
Not unless you count football, no. Some pretty passionate encounters, though; none more than the 1974 end-of-season game which Hartlepool won 1–0, sealing Hull's relegation. The goal was backheeled by ex-Hull hero Malcolm 'Super' MacDonald. The match was abandoned five minutes early when Hull fans rioted. A mounted policeman on a white horse restored order almost single-handedly.

What happened to Hull?
Ground closed for the first four games of next season, but promoted at the first attempt. They stormed to the top through a combination of shirt magnate Sir Terry Tootal's money and the inspiration of Messianic manager and ex-Tigers' keeper, 'Wor' Kevin Keelan. He was lucky to make the interview, having been attacked as he slept in a lay-by on the way up.

Not by Hartlepool fans, surely?
No. Hartlepool fans were still buoyant after their shock triumph the year before, when they conquered the mighty Leeds to win the FA Cup for the first time since 1937.

WOR KEV! . . . Keelan, that is, getting discount on a natty jacket in a Hartlepool boutique

Heady days in the north-east then?
For a while. But then fish wars with Norway impoverished Hartlepool, while Tootal's revolutionary 'Everlast' fabric was exposed as a sham on TV by Sir Alec Guiness. The company folded; players weren't paid, gates were locked, creditors swarmed and fans' favourite Roy Race was sold to raise money.

Did the clubs unite in hardship?
Grow up! Hull fans would taunt Hartlepool with fish (mainly mackerel, they called them the 'mackems'). Hartlepool fans would respond by waving their shirts over their heads, singing 'gotta shirt, gotta shirt, gotta shirt'.

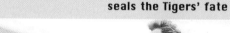

SUPERMAC! . . . Ex-Hull hero Macdonald seals the Tigers' fate

So what happened?
Both clubs were added to the growing Sports 'n' Leisure portfolio of Sir Eric 'Canny Monster' Hall of Newcastle United. Hull became the Humberside Hyenas, a struggling softball outfit, while Hartlepool mutated into rounders also-rans, the Stockton Rockets.

There used to be a saying: 'If it ain't broke, don't fix it.' But no one ever took much notice, so the last 100 years or so have seen intermittent tinkering with football's rules. Documents recently released by the Pan-Galactic FA show the 'thinking' behind some of the landmark changes. This fax shows the motivation behind some early-century alterations.

MOVING THE GOALPOSTS
Part One

FROM: Owtsperhan Orrinj Brayerburn Apell, Advertising Inc

TO: FIFA HQ

RE: SOCCER RELAUNCH, 2001

Guys! Hi!
Preliminary thoughts re your anxieties as expressed at the last meet. Don't have a cow if these shoes don't fit. It's a working draft not tablets of stone, so, like the man says, read, digest, consider, communicate. Let's go to work.

1. GOAL-COUNT
Okay, you did the post-thing, then you did the crossbar-thing. Now you got 3.022 goals per game average worldwide instead of 2.788. So sedate my raging heart. It's fractions, fellas, and decimal points don't put fannies on plastic. Get lateral with this. Problem: Brazil 2 Germany 1. Might be a helluva game but it sounds lame. Solution: Brazil 4 Germany 3. Same game, same goals, but Brazil score two from outside the box, which gets 2 x 2, and Fritz and the guys pop one in from 30 metres plus – it's a big three-er. Think of the permutations: half a goal extra if the guy scores with his weaker foot, whatever. Done this way, could be Brazil 4 ³/4 Germany 3 ¹/2. Much more sexy. Enough stats and the baseball-nerds'll be all over you like cold sores (and those guys spend dollars, not dimes). Remember: sometimes the product's fine, it just needs to come in a cuter box.

2. THE RULE STUFF

• Offside: Yeah yeah, you told us. It's like a religion with you guys, but respecting your sincerity and all, IT SUCKS! IT'S BORING! IT'S HARD TO FIGURE! And people just HATE IT when the guy's running at the goalie all on his own with the ball at his feet and the wind in his hair and the crowd roars and rises and suddenly the little flag-guy's waving it and the ref blows his whistle AND THE WHOLE THING HAS TO STOP AND START AGAIN GOING THE OTHER WAY! Think about it: if offside didn't exist and we suggested it, you'd assume you were victims of a giant pud-pull, right? So, do what you got to, paint a line, make a new zone, build a fence, whatever; but trash it before it trashes you.

• Direct or indirect free kick: Hey, who cares?

• Throw-ins: the guy has yet to be born who can do one of these without looking a total wuss. What is it, some kind of 'netball' thing? If you really don't go for kicks, how about a single-arm side-slinger goalie-type thing? i) you get the distance, and ii) throwing like that automatically makes the player look like a Greek guy in a statue with a discus or something.

3. TIME-FRAME AND FORMAT

Some polarities: over here, 18-30 yrs average TV attention span is 17.35 seconds; in England cricket lasts five days and no one wins. Best of both these crazy worlds is five 20-minute chunks, each separated by five minutes and each with a maximum two time-outs per team. Aside from getting the adsellers all icky with buck-lust, it means we got a basic end-to-end 120 min package, with top and tail OB and chat and slo-mo to take us up to the killer four hours. Bulk equals weight; substance begets substance, fellas. Plus, it's just whispers and rumours right now, but the long-term word is PTOs (Paid Time-Outs). Big bucks'll mean you can pull the big TO just when your goalie's on his ass and their guy's about to slip it in. Money buys the best players, why not the best playing conditions also? Go figure.

We'll talk soon.

Ciao for now.

The Guys.

Amusing pranks or the skinny end of a subversive wedge? Breakthroughs in Time-Travel mean it's available to more people than ever. But freedom brings responsibility, and it's clear that a hooligan element is using Time-Travel for destructive ends. The Finchley Five case has made clear the scale of the danger to football. Five clever, devious young nihilists, armed with extra-strong doses of Narcoleptica, were able to go back in time and spread chaos, unpicking vital stitches all over football history's vast woolly jumper.

EXHIBIT ONE: **WORLD CUP FINAL, WEMBLEY 1966**

One of their boldest stunts, the Five's attempt to induce sleep in the England team foundered on the side's adrenaline-levels. 'That was what did for us,' admitted ringleader Trevor Tuffin, 'we were still experimenting with doses.' As the picture shows, it nearly worked. Martin Peters wrote in his autobiography: 'Hursty came over all funny. Not so much knackered, but tired, bedtime tired. Shep [England physio] was sponging his face, going "Wake up, boy! Wake up!" Hursty was saying "Want me jimmy-jams. Time for bye-byes." I just ignored him. Mooro was wobbly too, one minute he's up, giving it Captain Courageous, next he's on his backside.' And though Jack Charlton (No.5) had the neck of a giraffe and the heart of a horse, even he nearly succumbed. 'I remember really fancying a hot milky drink,' he recalled, 'and I asked Alf to bring us a blanket. He told us not to be so bloody daft.'

EXHIBIT TWO: **FA CUP FINAL, WEMBLEY 1970**

Tuffin told the court how Narcoleptica was administered via a poison dart to the ring finger of Billy Bremner's left hand (see photo). The Leeds skipper was about to take a throw when he suddenly sank to his knees and appeared to start snoring. Don Revie swore his team to secrecy in case opponents were buoyed by evidence of his team's fallibility. 'We were that close,' said Tuffin, 'another 20 seconds and not even Norman Hunter's boot up his arse would have woken him.'

EXHIBIT THREE: **EUROPEAN CUP FINAL, WEMBLEY 1968**

'Of course,' smirked Tuffin, 'there's no way we can tell how an individual might react when he's out

for the count.' This line of defence was sufficient to convince the court not to press charges of Incitement to Displays of Public Lewdness. 'We just knock 'em out,' Tuffin continued, 'little Nobby Stiles, see, him and the big geezer on his left, they're spark out. All we did was make 'em fall asleep, what they get up to after that, that's their business, isn't it?'

TIME BANDITS!

EXHIBIT FOUR: FA CUP FINAL, VILLA v MAN U, WEMBLEY 1957

During the trial, Tuffin and his cohorts confirmed the authorities' worst fears: no agenda, no pattern, no axe to grind with any club or country. Trevor's twin, Tommy, explained: 'If there's a statement, it's that there is no statement. Clubs, colours, songs, anthems, once you get into all that, you may as well jump in the freezer with the rest of the vegetables. If you're looking for clues, the clue is chaos!' The

point was never better made than in the sabotage of the 1957 Cup final. It was always maintained that United's keeper, Wood (prone in photo), was injured in collision with Villa's McParland. But Wood actually fell swiftly asleep, and McParland slipped on something he's just smelt on his hand (Wembley was a public common for dog-walkers and picnickers until 1978). Quizzed as to why they'd picked this match, Tommy Tuffin shrugged. 'Why not?' he sneered.

EXHIBIT FIVE: CHARLTON ATHLETIC v BOCA JUNIORS, TOKYO 2004

The notorious 'Tokyo Nap Massacre' was almost certainly the Five's 'finest' hour. The World Cup Championship final was reduced to farce as six Boca Juniors were reduced to a penalty-area snooze midway through the second half. But Charlton's unfancied heroes weren't about to argue. They defended the goal pinched in the six-yard box siesta and won 2–1. Boca keeper, Barrafuego, is seen clinging to the net, beginning an ascent which ended when he collapsed in the hammock-like

comfort of the roof of the net. When the plot was uncovered, Charlton were asked, but refused, to return the trophy. 'We won it fair and square,' said boss Alan Curbishley, 'you can only beat the men on the park, it don't matter if their lads fall asleep, the game's still there to be won.'

They called it . . .

'HUMOUR'

Funny. Funny-ha-ha. Fun-neee. DR SKORN – half-computer, half-Vulcan – defines the anatomy of a football 'side-splitter'.

1. TIMELESS HUMOUR

Just as Egyptologists were able to use certain key hieroglyphs to eventually unlock the mysteries of the pyramids, likewise the soccerologists of today employ examples of timeless humour in our quest to decipher the meaning of all ancient football humour. The 'Rosetta Stone' of our science was the eternally amusing 'Football Coach' gag, which played a pivotal role in revealing the humour inherent in permed hair, Jeff Astle's singing career, 'Julian Dicks' and pictures of players when they were slightly younger.

a. No Football Coaches Admitted

'Yesterday, I was driving my automobile on the motorway when I decided to stop for refreshments at a service-station. There, I saw a sign which I considered a little unfair on Don Howe: it said "No Football Coaches Admitted"!'

b. Football Coaches Pt. 2

Q: When is a football coach not a football coach?
A: When he turns into (England physiotherapist) Fred Street!
NB: This timeless gag may still require a little work.

2. ORAL HUMOUR

Ecologically sensible 'jokes' were regularly recycled at the expense of interchangeable players or teams.

a. What Time Does the Match Start?

A (Wimbledon) supporter telephones the club-line at (Selhurst Park), asking 'What time does the match start?' The voice at the other end responds: 'What time can you get here, sir?' *Correct response:* 'Ho ho. Good one.'

b. The Sofa

I hear (Notts County) have a new Main Stand. It is, in fact, a three-seater settee.

3. WORDPLAY

A more advanced form of oral humour.

a. Centaur Forward

A Greek mythic creature, half-man and half-horse, is wearing a football jersey. A recognisable football manager figure introduces the non-existent beast thus: 'He's our new centaur forward.' *Explanation:* 'centaur forward' sounds (phonetically) similar to 'centre forward' – a witty football position pun.

b. He's Lost His Head

The dual meaning of the phrase, 'He's lost his head and kicked it over the bar!' induced mirth when coupled with a literal cartoon drawing of this unlikely event.

4. TERRACE HUMOUR

Most effective when shouted at great volume at opportune moments during a match. Pre-prepared similarly to oral 'jokes', but always delivered as if original and/or spontaneous, terrace humour was for some time inaccurately categorised as a 'Humour of Response'. *Note:* Sit down, you puff!?!

a. The Terrace Test

Try to work out what on-field action or primary terrace humour may have acted as a cue for the following witticisms: 1) 'He got there as quickly as he was able'; 2) 'He could not catch a cold'; 3) 'He resembles the team manager in that he has a bad side'.

b. The Amusing Threat

A goal scored against the team favoured by one group of football supporters triggered a popular comedy forewarning to their rivals: 'You are going home in a flashing ambulance.' The consequential quitting of the ground ten minutes before final whistle was known as 'the Humour of Anticipation'.

5. VISUAL HUMOUR

a. Fowler The Goldfish

Likening players to animals induced mirth. Especially if the animal was a goldfish.

b. The Child in the Hat

Children's football magazines would print the same cartoon joke on a regular basis, preparing their readership for the cyclical nature of grown-up football humour. This was known as 'the Humour of Recognition'. *Example:* A man enters a turnstile, wearing an oversize 'top' hat in club colours. Upon closer inspection, two small holes can be seen to have been drilled in the hat. Within earshot of the club official, a voice from inside the hat says, 'Are we in yet, dad?'

CHEAP JIBE Gazza in his digs

CHEAP JIBE Babbman and Robin Redknapp clash over Ryan Giggs's girlfriend, Pussywoman

6. THE CHEAP JIBE

See annotated graphical examples, you overweight bespectacled cuckold!

7. THE PUZZLE OF 'RUDE' HUMOUR

a. 'Barbwa Windsor's bikini!?! Pwoi-oi-oing!?!'

Human males once found certain bodily appendages and functions more hilarious than others. This football team, compiled entirely of players with amusing biological names, appeared in a fan-magazine of the mid-1990s, where its appearance was hailed as a pinnacle of comic achievement. The annotation following individual player names was not part of the original article, but was added by myself at a later date for the illumination of my specialist 'Toilet Humour' students.

Appendix:
CARRY-ON OO-ERNITED!?!
Meet the Double (entendre)-winners . . .

1. PERRY SUCKLING
Not to be confused with our Comedy Druggie XI's goalkeeper, Perry Digweed.

2. EINAR AAS
Nottingham Forest's Scandinavian import is a confusing entry, his name being pronounced 'Orse' rather than the higher-potential 'Arse'. Surviving videotape of half-time summariser 'Greavsie' sheds little light on the mystery. After watching a series of clips showing the player losing out in the tackle, the expert made the high-comic response: 'Looks to me like he dunno his Orse from his elbow.'

3. OSCAR ARCE
Apparently only of passing amusement to Aston Villa fans of the 1960s, who were sufficiently cosmopolitan to know the Argentinian's name was most likely pronounced 'Ar-chay', 'Ar-say' or 'Ar-thay' – even though everyone at the time pronounced Ajax as if it were a sink-scourer. True 'bathroom' jollity was only prompted by Villa manager Vic Hallam's habit of putting Arce on the teamsheet directly above . . .

4. BARRY HOLE

5. DAVID BUSST
Coventry City's popular bosom-pun central-defender. Reportedly, fan-magazine readers were disappointed to discover that the Sky-Browns snapped up Busst not from Bristol Rovers or Bristol City but from the French club Breste. So he was not 'cup'-tied. Though he was quite a handful up front, etc., etc.

6. WAYNE WANKLIN
Reading. The 1970s. The first co-ordinates punched into the time-machine controls of thousands of modern-day football fans on my 'Heckling For Beginners' course. An average Reading gate of 5,000 in 1979 is now reckoned to have included up to 1,500 time-travelling Wayne-baiters disguised in museum-piece 'bovver' apparel.

7. ADRIAN LITTLEJOHN
Here, a pun can be made on the vernacular for 'small penis', as in journalist 'Dick' of the *Daily Mail*.

8. JIM BONE
Ex-Partick and Norwich, currently 'making it big' as St Mirren manager.

9. MIKE TREBILCOCK
Was Portsmouth's 1965 Cup-winning hat-trick hero just boasting about the length of his hi-ho Pompey, or was he in fact afflicted with three of the blighters? Either way, lucky old Mrs Trebilcock came out of the deal smiling.

10. DEAN WINDASS

11. GLADSTONE SMALL

Manager: SID JAMES
Heritage Secretary: VIRGINIA BOTTOMLEY
Home Ground: Groundshare with Millwall. At COLD BLOW LANE!?!

SKILL IN SPACE

Take a Trip to Planet Tip-top Tip. But remember. It's not the winning, it's the taking rock samples that matters . . .

THE INTERGALACTIC NUTMEG

Do not attempt to take on any alien player without first counting his total number of legs. If the total comes to greater than two, your plans for an attempted 'nutmeg' should be swiftly revised.

PUT SOME SNOW ON IT

Good interpersonal communication is vital to any team's progress. But playing in space, the days of 'Goalie's ball' and 'Man/creature on!' are long past. A casual observer of this on-pitch communication schematic might notice that the players all appear to have their heads set way off to one side. But any football tactician would instantly recognise the fabulous Nexus

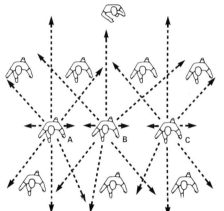

5 team of season 2016–17, who swept the whole universe before them thanks to their groundbreaking use of CB radio – precursor of the standard in-helmet footballphone used today.

See how each Nexus player was linked to the others by a handset trapped between their ear and shoulder. Only the goalkeeper's primitive on-field system appears to be less than fully operational: he can be seen placing a quick call to the Nexus club-line to find out the current state of play.

GOALIES FROM PLANET SLIMEBALL

The WFA recommend that Earth teams refrain henceforth from employing journeyman goalkeepers from Planet Slimeball. As in the 1990s case of netmen imported to England from Australia and America, Slimeballian qualifications stand for little in the higher

standard of non-glutinous football played on Earth. Employ a jelly-monster custodian at your peril. Jelly-monster custodians are rubbish. Do not be fooled by a promising-sounding goalie animal nickname (William 'Spider' Butterfingers, Erik 'The Kat' Dropsvedt), a backpack crammed full of minor interplanetary caps or a hefty intergalactic price-tag. Once again, that official WFA word on the big KY lads: they are rubbish.

DALEK TACTICAL INVASION 2150AD

In Fig. 1 dalek OL splits a zonal defence by trundling to the by-line and pulling the ball back for dalek IL to head for goal. In Fig. 2 dalek IR endeavours to beat his opposing white dalek left-half, draws a second defender out of position and then passes to an unmarked black dalek colleague, offering a quickly taken shot.

Or maybe those things look more like keyholes than daleks.

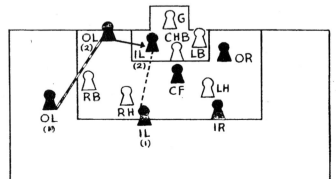

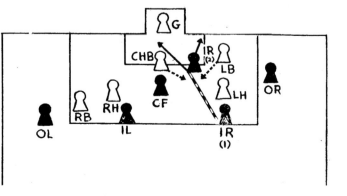

a trip to
PLANET HARD

Formerly plain old Stavonix C9, since the Pan-Galactic FA decided Transportation was the cure to the sickness of indiscipline, this unremarkable sphere in the Outer Reaches has been better known to fans as Planet Nutter, Planet Sin-Bin or simply Planet Hard. Anxious now to shed its grim image, and with a name-change to help, the governors of 'Reformia' asked THE TREASURY over to see what kind of progress the colony was making.

GETTING THERE

Increasingly easy. ReformAir offers a range of tickets to suit most budgets; flights or Time Compressions to Ince InterGlobal are available from most Galactic Termini. If your stay includes Saturday night the price will increase; expect to be asked for blood and urine specimens and evidence of a conviction-free history.

ON ARRIVAL

You should bear in mind that Reformia (they hate to hear it called Planet Hard these days) no longer actively encourages the sort of behaviour that might spring to mind when you first think of it. So, no in-flight fighting or food-throwing, no hilarious antics on the baggage reclaim carousel, no fire-extinguisher fun in Customs, and strictly no vomiting in the back of your SpacePort taxi.

THE LOCALS

Remember, just about everyone on Reformia is either a Disciplinee or a Disciplinee's descendant. So in conversation with locals try to avoid sweeping statements, especially if you've a tendency to be judgemental. For example, 'Leopards don't change their spots', 'He'd never kick another ball in his life if I had my way' and 'Hanging's too good for 'em' may all be expressions to avoid, at least until you've nurtured a rapport between the two of you. Plump instead for something more along the line of 'I always say there's a little bit of good in all of us', 'It's society's fault, isn't it?', 'There's too much money in the game these days' or 'It's the price you pay for genius'.

ENTERTAINMENTS

Reformia's problem is to attract tourism without scaring off visitors with its reputation. For this reason, an awful lot of repackaging and rewriting of history's gone on. Those once considered thuggish are now styled as 'colourful characters', cheats are 'loveable rogues' and the plainly psychotic remodelled as 'mavericks'. Diversions on Reformia largely consist of sanitised versions of the past, so why not try some of the many available themed events and games? Play Taxi Queue or Last Man Standing with Big Duncan, go for spot-cash prizes in Win a Tenner, Stare at Keaney, or try your hand at Clubbing with Gazza or Pizza with the Arsenal. Most of these are included in the price of the more popular packages.

SPEAKING THE LANGUAGE

Depending on the reasons for your visit, you might want to bear in mind some indigenous customs and traditions, ignorance of which could lead to – in local parlance – 'the whole thing kicking off'. Questions such as 'What are you looking at?', 'Want some, do ya?' or 'Did you spill my pint?' are purely rhetorical. Eye-contact with locals should generally be kept to a minimum. Call nobody 'mate', 'pal', 'chummy' or 'sport' unless specifically invited to.

GUIDED TOURS

The authorities have cleverly turned adversity to their advantage and created sites of special interest and memorial areas. Of the areas we visited, we thought Battytown retained a lingering aura of authentic menace but lacked variety, while Hunter-on-the-Hill was a rather whimsical and overdone 'English village' which recreated the period charms of the 1970s. Dicksyland was altogether too lifelike and frightening for the children in THE TREASURY's party, so we're unable to report on it fully.

ANDERTON'S HOUSE

A popular draw during our stay appeared to be the House of Darren 'Grizzly' Anderton. This was a moving exhibition which demonstrated via pictures, video and interactivity the remarkable changes 'The Hitman' underwent prior to his Transportation in 2013. Early exhibits confirm he started as a gifted ball-player with a leggy, oddly graceful style, a fabulous peachy complexion and the saucy but winning grin of an agreeably cheeky 'paper boy'. Subsequent exhibits record his transfer to Manchester United, his use as 'anchor-man' in England's doomed 1998 World Cup campaign and his eventual transformation into the awesome 'Silent Assassin' or 'Killer Gazelle' of early-century legend.

THE TREASURY'S VERDICT

Clearly much work has been put in by Reformia's governors, but a new start takes more than a nice new livery, some theme-rides and a change of name. Cheers

for the flights and hotels and mini-bars and everything, ReformAir, but might we make a few suggestions? Thanks:

1. If there's to be an entire Battytown surely you can muster a similarly scaled tribute to Big Jim Baxter? We could, for a small consideration, let you see our plans for Baxborough.

2. You *must must must* label more clearly and frankly the horrors behind the walls of not just Dicksyland but also the Sounesseria. Children could be permanently damaged.

3. Howzabouta fun-for-the-kids all-star celebrity Jan 'n' Tone Theme Dodgems?

4. The Fash's Elbow Russian Roulette Ride is positively dangerous and, if our party's experience is anything to go by, the risk of facial disfigurement is substantially higher than one in six. You'll be hearing from our legal people.

THE GREATEST-EVER ALL-TIME
IRELAND XI!

1. PATRICK
U2. GELDOF
3. O'BRIEN
4. PREDATOR
5. MANDELA
6. DOONICAN
7. JUNINHO
8. GILES
9. YEBOAH
10. BEST
11. LOGAN
Manager: Jack CHARLTON

1. Saint PATRICK

Paddy was the ace custodian who single-handedly rid Ireland of snakes. A safe pair of hands if ever there was one, to be sure.

U2. Fifi Trixibelle GELDOF

Hundreds of injured footballers still flock every year to the Dublin bachelor flat where FT's father Saint Bob invented the life-saving Band Aid sticking plaster. As lead-singer of the hopeless leather-trousered pop group U2, he later went on to invent punk rock, stadium rock and art rock, just five or six years after everybody else. On the ball, Fifi shows all the invention of her father, plus the overlapping positional skills of Bob's up-front striking partner, the cheeky flanker Paula Yates.

3. Chief O'BRIEN

Chief O'Brien out of *Star Trek: The Next Generation* shone like a dilithium crystal on the left side of defence in this year's thrilling FU Cup final defeat. A trusty intergalactic up-and-downer, Chief O'Brien is noted for his, ahem, good engine.

4. PREDATOR

The hard-tackling dreadlocked monster lad got the Irish call from Big Jack the day after he was shot in the gut by Arnold Schwarzenegger, and proved to have green blood.

PREDATOR Hoolit

5. Nelson MANDELA

Jack Charlton wasted no time in calling up this well-respected elder statesman of the game as soon as the details of his Irish qualification were confirmed by 50,000 football fans at Dublin Airport – to the tune of 'We Are Going Up'. All together now: 'Ooh-ah Paul McGrath's da / I said Oo-ah Paul McGrath's da . . .'

6. Val DOONICAN

A calming influence on any back line, smooth operator Doonican was noted for his ability to shackle any forward. Usually to his trademark bar-stool, planted firmly in the mud 30 yards from goal.

7. JUNINHO

Snapped up for his country on the basis that any player who hasn't got a first name must be a bit of all right, the Brazilian Teessider was deemed eligible to play for Ireland because he regularly passed through (or was that near?) Irish airspace on his regular trips home to the slums of Rio. At the time of publication, Juninho still only looks about 12 years old.

8. Johnny GILES

Rated by many as one of the finest European football minds, history has been kind to Giles: everyone in 2097 has completely forgotten his role as terrorist in a certifiably psychopathic Leeds team, which was somewhat eclipsed by the less sneaky misconduct of Bremner, Hunter, Charlton, Yorath, McQueen and Revie.

9. Tony YEBOAH

Previously thought to be Ghanaian, the question of Mr Constrictor's nationality was finally cleared up with the assistance of All-Time Ireland's manager Jack

FOODIE-OMETER
READING:
17 lagers, 1 egg
sarnie, sir! (see
'Food is Trendy')

Charlton – he flew to Paris with his shock documentation, treated FIFA bloke Joe Havelunch to a judicious night on the tiles, and hung on to the pictures. Havelunch later confirmed Yeboah was admissible because when he first moved to Leeds, his landlady Mrs Butterworth was looking after her Uncle Aidan's Irish wolfhound.

10. George BEST

All-Time Best??? 'We'd try to organise a situation where I got a bird in bed and the rest watched from wardrobes or behind curtains or whatever. There was nothing dirty in it – it was just a big laugh for the lads. We charged 50p each for that. The girls never knew, and I'd have screwed them in any case, so what's the difference?'

11. Johnnie LOGAN

Record-breaking double Eurovision Cup-winner Johnnie makes the All-Time Irish XI despite the fact that no one can remember either of his victorious songs, despite his stiffest opposition coming from Bucks Fizz, and despite the fact that he was actually Australian. Sign him up, Mr Charlton!

QUARTER-FINAL HIGHLIGHTS

FOOTBALL UNIVERSE CUP 2097

THE DALEKS v THE MEKON

Match abandoned after 17 minutes

Controversy raged as the two most evil sides left in the competition were expelled for persistent foul play. After a quarter of an hour the Daleks were already down to six men for attempted exterminations. The Mekon was so evil he was down to one man from the kick-off, thus failing to get on the end of some of his own useful crosses and capitalising on his understandable aerial dominance.

The final straw came for the Vulcan referee when none of the remaining Daleks proved willing to take a regulation throw-in, with the ball passing fully over their head. Logically, the game could not continue.

'We're well gutted,' commented Dalek captain Davros. 'But then I s'pose even if our names had been on the cup this year we'd never have made it up them flippin' Wembley steps. Some afternoons it's like the whole universe is against you, Barry.'

STAR TREK 1
UFO 0

Despite bossing the match through their purple-haired dolly-bird midfield, the string-vests flopped badly in front of goal. Maybe it was a mistake to play their Interceptor pilots up front: those funny little helicopter things have only got one big bullet sticking out the front, so after every shot the strikeforce had to return to Moonbase for more midfield ammo.

Mr Chekhov scored the Trekkies a free bye to the final with a second-half warp drive from fully 25 light years.

THE MEKON Useful in the air, but uncomfortable with the ball played in to feet . . .

189

HALL OF FAME

Scarabula C

To some a hero, to others the evilest agent of darkness ever to contaminate our game with the touch of a septic tentacle, Scarabula C's presence in our marbled Hall of Fame will cause controversy. Surely, his adherents will say, his place is secure if only because of his extraordinary goal-scoring feats at trans-Galactic level. With equal vehemence, his millions of detractors will point to a disciplinary record of unparalleled shame, to the episodes of stimulant abuse and to the cheating, kicking, intimidation and decadence of his long and ugly career.

To understand this furore more clearly, we should understand, perhaps, that Scarabula C hails from that dark and squalid corner of the Universe called the Xermine Cluster, where life is cheap and honour an unknown concept. For the tiny Scarabula C, growing up in the Cluster's southernmost hovels, only football could match the twin prizes of escape and prosperity offered by space-piracy.

His debut for the Cluster's Youth XI in 2055 held in microcosm the coming shape of his career. Two brilliant first-quarter goals, a running feud with the opposition sweeper, a violent time-out spat with his manager, removing and urinating on his captain's armband and, finally, a two-tentacle lunge at a linesman who disallowed his third 'goal'.

But throughout his career there was no shortage of owners willing to pay for his wayward genius. NewsCorp EurAsia, Mid-Venus III, Atletico Pluto and SonyMars FC all burnt their fingers trying to handle the hot moon-potato he became. His football genius was matched only by a self-destructive streak as wide as the Sea of Tranquility, and on every improbable goal hung a price tag of an abandoned baby, too much pie or space-carts drunkenly crashed.

But Scarabula C will be best remembered – and most reviled – for his part in SonyMars' winning goal in the Trans-Solar semis in 2070. No one knows how the referee failed to spot his anterior tentacles coiled around the legs of Mid-Earth's keeper at that last-minute corner. Allegations of rigging survive to this day, but nothing alters the fact that Janet Seaman could neither jump nor move, and in the ensuing melee a Martian boot scuffed the ball home. Scarabula C compounded the fury of millions of mid-Earthers by describing his filthy Xermine stranglehold on brave Janet as 'a token of my love for the people of the Earth'. Mid-Earthers may not be alone in wishing that the young Scarabula C had heeded his mother's advice and remained a space-pirate. The conditions and pay compare favourably, and he wouldn't have been voted 'Most Loathed Space Alien Ever' by subscribers to FootMail Earth for eight consecutive years.

Scarabula C's back in the Cluster again now – where he belongs, some might say – where it's rumoured he sells narcotics to the young and simple-minded.

They called it . . . 'SEX'

GIRL OF THE MATCH

Soccerologists agree that the 'Girl of the Match' page from Coventry City's 'Sky Blue' match-day magazine may hold the key to the long-forgotten sexual attitudes of football fans in the 1970s.

At every home fixture, a single female would be selected, photographed and presented for partial bodily monitoring. Soccer-ology is now split over the vexed question of why this phenomenon occurred. Also how, given zero biographical input, zero personality data and a marked absence of statistical parameters, fans were expected to select and nominate a 'best' contestant. Logically, this was an impossible task. Insufficient information. Does Not Compute.

Witness the female pictured seated in a motor-car. Few objective facts are available. Her dress has 'ridden up' so her pants are clearly visible. Her semi-random 'good'ness value has been estimated by modern-day experts to be the square root of 534.33 recurring.

Witness the female partially dissolved in a blue fluid. Historical research tells us her 'bikini-brassiere' was named in honour of a nuclear explosion on the Pacific atoll of Brassiere. The garment is formed from a fabric called 'cheese-cloth'. With all other variables un-fixed and inderterminable, the excellence quotient assigned is a nominal 34B.

The historical mystery deepens in the 1990s. Despite the growth of the 'feminist' movement – so logically opposed to the wantonly random display of cheese-cloth – popular football fanzines now delighted in reprinting the newly offensive portraits of the 'Highfield Road martyrs'. One

key soccerological text, a football nostalgia treasury, even saw fit to drag its available 'Girl of the Match' material over three rather desperate sex-related pages.

What could have been the popular fascination with these females and their attendant insoluble puzzle?

SOCCEROLOGY PUZZLE

Now is your opportunity to participate in an important soccerological survey. Simply study the six females on the original competition entry-form – in the interests of football science. Consider on what possible basis football fans from the Dark Ages were supposed to pick the 'best' Girl of the Match. Experts have narrowed the possibilities down to six: order them in terms of probable correctness. If you think you know better than the finest football minds of 2097, add your own pathetic amateurish guess in the space provided.

Dear Dr Skorn,
I claim my free gift sky-blue elephant ash-tray set.
I think Cov's caveman fans voted for their favourite 'Girl of the Match' on the strength of . . .

1. The length of rope dangling from their head
2. How many Pacific islands got a namecheck in their clothing
3. How many dairy-based foodstuffs got a namecheck in their clothing
4. How many 'pedalo' pleasure-boats were visible behind them on the horizon
5. Something else to do with that rope
6. Or maybe something to do with statues in the background
Other...

SAMMY SPACE CADET SAYS: If you couldn't care less how **Girl of the Season 1972** was picked, why not just put the girls in order of **sexy belly buttons**!?! Win a **winter sunshine holiday for two** if your 1–6 matches Dr Skorn's!?!

THREE: Bobby Charlton v Nobby Charmer

CASE IN BRIEF: In a hushed atmosphere of great respect, evidence was heard of the remarkable Robert 'Bobby' Charlton: of his then record 106 games for England, and of 49 goals, unmatched until Robbie Fowler's 50th in 2006. In addition, between 1956 and 1973, Charlton scored a record 198 goals in 606 games for Manchester United. If such feats were not extraordinary enough, they were achieved in a manner at once amenable, courteous and brave. Not for Bobby the underhand brutalities practised elsewhere during his career, in, say, South America, continental Europe or West Yorkshire.

Nobby Charmer, his backers suggested, was the only Machine able to rival the esteemed Sir Bobby. They certainly wouldn't base their case on the destruction of Charlton's; his credentials remained unassailed. Charlton's team thanked them for their courtesy; Charmer's said not at all, it was the least they could do. The Symposium asked if we could please get on.

Charmer, they were told, had been created by Matsushita Inc not just to win matches, but also to 'put a smile back on the face of galactic football'. Care had been taken to omit from his blueprint any trace of disloyalty, malice or arrogance. Computers fed with the data had come up with a design similar to Charlton himself. Charmer also, the Symposium heard, packed a fair old shot, though a lovable 'homely' accent had proved beyond the design team's voice reproduction capabilities.

RELEVANT DATA: The Symposium was reminded by his team of Charlton's extraordinary career; Charmer's backers had to be silenced when their standing ovation moved into its third minute. As well as the raw facts of his excellence, it was pointed out that Charlton helped pioneer the role of the deep-lying forward, and that his gentlemanly demeanour was a force for good not just for England abroad, but also for a Manchester United team not without its hot-headed talents. Testimony from Georgie 'Best' was heard that had it not been for Charlton, he wouldn't have enjoyed such a long and productive career.

In response, Nobby Charmer's team offered no evidence, insisting, to the Symposium's clear irritation, that to do so would be to slander the great man's name.*

CONTEXT: It had been hard, his team said, for Charlton to establish his reputation when the public often couldn't help but associate him with his big-necked big brother. Jackie, the Symposium heard, over-compensated for the stigma of being named after a girls' periodical by 'doing' the names in his 'little black book', by jigging about in front

So revered by fellow pros they would queue for the privilege of carrying him!

* His team made it a condition of our coverage that no photos of Charmer be included, as to show his image on the same page as Lord Bob would be 'a travesty and a slight on the great man'.

of goalkeepers at corners and by playing for the deeply unpopular Leeds United. Little Bobsy, by contrast, turned out for the gloriously cavalier Red Devils, the 'most famous team in the whole world'. (At this point, even Charmer's side was moved to object; the Symposium sustained the objection, urging Charlton's team not to push its luck.) As well as this cruel surname handicap, Bobby had been compelled to hear the same lame joke about his hair for most of his life.

Charmer's team (in 20th-century parlance) 'held up their hands' to that, and added that Charmer hadn't had the tough north-east mining background to break away from, either. Charlton's side wished this added to their case, conceding they'd not thought of it. Charmer's team again mounted no substantial opposition to Saint Bob, though did make it clear that Charmer was not in the habit of lamenting the passing of National Service every time football-related disorder broke out on screen.

SIR BOB...So good, this was probably a goal!

VERDICT: The Symposium felt the need for some strong drink and rough company for a couple of days. On returning a verdict, they decided in favour of Nobby Charmer, just for the hell of it. Charmer's team appealed, claiming Charlton was a much better player and a far nicer man, and that they'd represented Charmer only because they'd been forced to and because the fees were so generous. The Symposium overturned their own decision, awarded the verdict to Charlton and ordered all costs to be met by Charmer's team.

BLACK SHEEP GIRAFFE! . . . Throwing his weight around like a big bully again!

By the middle of the century the game was changing too fast for FIFA. The Pan-Galactic FA took over and announced new guidelines for a new age ('The New Football'), an age that would include non-Earthly life-forms. It took soundings from around the Galaxy, and the following e-mail represents perhaps the single most influential contribution to the debate.

MOVING THE GOALPOSTS
Part Two

TO: Havela@pangalfa.footnet.mars

FROM: SoccCom@jupefa.uninet.jupe

MadamSirs,

To find herewith numerous of suggestings and/or planthoughts toward 'The New Football', as in your words.

1. MEMBERS
Please – this is to talk not of members in a clubship way, but members so to speak arm, leg and general limb-age. So for this cause we say:

i) it must be put in mind the tentacles, multi-limbed, several-headed and manifestly-footed. In the context of this perspective, for what is the referee to begin to whistle when comes the shout of 'handball', 'two-feeted tackle' or 'tackle from behind'? Indeed for the same matter, what can be a 'tackle from behind' when to a referee the frontness and behindicity is by no means a thing of clearness? We only and humbly ask.

ii) for satisfying all there ought be lines of guidance in re parts of players and with what can goals be scored, ball be struck etc. On the Earth we see players with a choosing limited to but two feet one head and no more. Such players will sustain grief and misbeknowings if against them play players with recourse to many more options of ball-striking. We seek no such hindrances to knowledge, only things of harmony.

2. VELOCITY FORCE AND SO ON
We here would seek to win many games without damage unduly unto adversaries. But problems are in the tubeline if some players in outlying dark space are to unleash shottage of maximum potency. These players have shot velocity quite without Earth boundaries; truly. Players there are there whose ball-strikes muster in excess of Earth 'bullet-train' speeds for comparative data. Might there not be some needs for such force in constraint? We think it; or injuries flow, for on our planet perhaps posts slightly go shake, but on Earth such shootings take from the goalkeeper the head from straight between his neckbones and, in your speaking, put it in row Z. Not a wound for spongebucket man to make fix.

3. TRADITIONAL RITUALISATIONS AND ETC

Here it would be for you to make with us some absolute reassurances. We have seen on the Earth some manners of making glee when ball finds goalnet. Truly, on our screens the Earth-men have fallen to the arms of one then the other, have coiled and roped, lip-hugging and spittle-wipes. This is not our tradition. Far away from it, to be frankly. Standards must set hard and fast also that Earth-players never with our or further outer-players make such falling and feeling and closeness. Miscomprehensions lie yonder down this street, and after miscomprehensions come twin-dogs of growly ignorance and then maybe fights. Not good, nor likely sought.

4. OFFSIDE

Of course, this law with us is also. Player closest goal but not keeper in the last pass is a defender or referee go whistle. Sure, this we have. But doubt's benefit must surely to attack, and to trot rearwards against play's run is also not to intercede in play. This is true for all, we think. We love this law, makes our planet happy. Once a year: National Offside Day, most hilarity; walk in street, to work, play, shopping, no matter; stranger can rush up waving longest arm over head and scream 'He's Off!'. At which nearest also stranger makes whistle noise and does award of 'free kick'. Person 'offside' then buy for stranger a sweetly or several. Just for fun! This way strangers make friends and larks to be had one and all.

5. REFEREES AND THE DISCIPLINE

We see on Earth screens of much and many spit and swear and shout and arguing. Here not so many. Here much times the Xalons come to ref. Not good for to make row with Xalon. Must be good also potential for agreements to cover shouting, kicking, pushing over, rudeness and such. Some of ours do these things, others do not, but we would request in partnership with Earth ceasings of such incordialities.

Jupiter seeks the friendships with Earth to play football and also not to play football. The peoples can make mingling and like to play the game. We many relish your comments to come on our comments just gone. If you speak Jupe better than our Earth, so for the gooder, if not, we try. Like they say in the pitch, many good lucks, and at day's final ending-part, the better team to make a win! (We can summon only 100 percentage in the park, truly you say!)

All our lovely regardments.

PETER SHILTON
and his
Amazing Gambling Muzzie!

Go on, have a flutter on two flies crawling up the wall with the poorest goalie in the universe.

Bet of the Century

Tarzan's running total stands at: minus one house, minus £2012.15 and minus three shirts.

Shilts' Form Guide: 'With the benefit of my amazing 147 years' memory – 131 of 'em in the top division – I'm going to give you lads the chance to make yourselves a few bob. Stick a tenner accumulator on this little lot in your old-fangled 1990s, and by the time you're my age you'll be as rich as my mate Keith Gillespie. In this old pros' home they only let us gamble with matchsticks, but no one can stop me betting against me debts! Stick the whole lot on for me, with the benefit of hindsight – dead-cert double or nothing!'

1. Melanie Griffiths' voice will one day be considered 'sexy'   250–1
2. Cov will have a 19-year run in the top division   500–1
3. Lee Evans will get his own TV show   1000–1
4. Someone other than Alan Shearer will score for Blackburn   250–1
5. Will Carling to shag Xxxx Xx   1000–1
6. Peter Shilton's muzzie to be written out of history by 2000   500–1

And your final money-doubling banker,

7. Either Sugar or Venables was telling the truth   Evens

Grand Total: Shilts scores minus two houses, minus ECU4024.30, minus six shirts . . . and counting.

Kevin Keegan's Kuddle Kolumn

Football's last great romantic makes a passionate plea from the past: 'Let's Have a Kwiet Night In . . .'

Hiya there in the future! Kevin Keegan here!

It doesn't matter whether it's 1977 or 2077, some things in this life will always remain konstant. One thing is that long hair will always be kool. Another thing is your ups and downs in football and in love.

It doesn't matter whether you're playing for Skunthorpe or some klub in space with an astroturf pitch, you'll always have injury worries, Kup upsets and skoring hikkups. Kevin Keegan says get your head down in training and think of it as a test of karakter.

But when it komes to love, things kan be a bit more komplikated. Romance and football have got these sticky patches in kommon, but you don't deal with them in kwite the same way. No way ho-zay.

Football lads of the future, if your relationship with your little lady has hit a rocky patch, the last thing you do is 50 times round the karpark. Take a tip from the great KK and take her out to a romantik bistro or brasserie. Let her have a starter as well as a main kourse. And why not go on to a show.

A giant padded kard and flowers will help put the sparkle back in your love-life. Do it like Kevin Keegan does it with his lovely wife Jean. Book up for an okkasional weekend in the kountryside or on the koast. Tell her she looks a million dollars in her new skirt.

Then when you want to go on tour with the lads she kan't kause a fuss.

EDISON SPEAK: A FOOT IN THE DOOR OF TIME

The Treasury's own door-stepping, time-travelling reporter beams back and forth through time to report live on pivotal moments in football's history . . .

Space Cadets, already they're calling this quite literally The Day The World Cup Died. Yesterday I had the proud privilege to witness first 'hand' the systematic destruction of Earth's finest. Their conquerors? Let's just say that among the scorers were the legendary likes of En-fka, Ionzor and the great, great Lingzit Q. That's right, today's Foot in the Door of Time comes fromt the year 2022 at the ColaDome, Tokyo, Japan, where China was 'smashed' 9–0 by a Galactic Select XI which arrived here unknown, unfancied and unwelcome, but which departs as quite possibly surely the most extraordinary team ever to play on this planet.

Make no mistake, Space Cadets, this lot from China were no mugs! This World Cup was a 'China' Cup just as overwhelmingly as the previous two; gargantuan against Ghana, immense against Italy and really good against Russia, they had fully ten Old Earth Days to recover from their exertions, and the Inter-Galactic Challenge was played at the venue, time and temperature of China's choosing. No, this was as fair and as square as it was awesome on the eye.

Shell-shocked Chinese team boss, Lee Chen, said later, 'Fair dos, they've done us for pace, technique, strength and control. We've gone out to boss it and impose ourselves as such, but to be fair, we've come second in every department. Ref's had a nightmare, mind. Ran the game like a sex pervert.'

But for me the Galactics merely toyed with a team who never fathomed how to win possession from their other-wordly opponents, toyed with them like a big nasty cat

might with a squeaky little mouse. Indeed, had 'Hands Across the Void' not been more important than 'Shots Across the Line', the enterprising outer-spacers might really have 'turned up the gas', 'stir-fried' the Chinese and left them quite literally 'steaming' on the eggfried rice of their Earthly limitations!

The game was a blur; the Galactics, six up by the break, added three more by the third quarter's end, and for the last quarter served a sumptuous picnic of keep-ball on a big fluffy blanket of skill; every flick a fresh-cut sandwich, every lay-off a fondant fancy, every one-two a deliciously sugary bun. A spellbound ColaDome rose to its feet for a ten-minute standing ovation; in their minds, this was the 'Real Thing!'. History in the making, Space Cadets, and your very own seat in the stands came courtesy of Edison Speak, putting my Foot in the Door of Time and reporting live for THE TREASURY.

END OF AN ERA . . . Opposing skippers, Deng-Huan Hoeness and The Mighty Ionzor, after the 2022 Inter-Galactic Challenge

FOOTBALL UNIVERSE CUP 2097

It's climax time! And in space, no one remembers the teams who get knocked out in the semis . . .

SEMI-FINALS

STAR TREK 2
BUCK ROGERS IN THE 25TH CENTURY 0

STAR TREK: THE NEXT GENERATION 2
JOSIE AND THE PUSSYCATS IN OUTER
SPACE 0

See what we mean? You've got to be a real Sammy Space Cadet to remember Josie and the Pussycats in Outer Space, let alone Luton Town in 1994 or the Teenage Mutant Ninja Turtles from '89.

CHEATING IS LOGICAL So *that's* how those Trekkies got to the final . . .

THE FINAL

STAR TREK 1
STAR TREK: THE NEXT GENERATION 0

From early morning, thousands of Trekkies crowded in fine humour along Wembley Way toward the hallowed twin towers and the wide open spaces of intergalactic football's Neutral Zone. Fans wearing 'Rooster' Picard wigs bantered with rival fans bedecked in ripped shirts and stage blood, each chanting their favourite classic excerpts of pompous dialogue.

With the Next Generation's big signing Worf cup-tied, having turned out for the Klingons in round one, all the pre-match talk was of the battle of the logical playmakers, Mr Spock versus Mr Data – the Vulcan mind-meld up against the might of positronic passing skills augmented by the tactical bonus of a bird who can read minds.

The ultimate local derby final kicked off amid some confusion as neither team was willing to change from their traditional mixed red, yellow and blue jerseys; but things got simpler after all the players in red who no one recognised got stretchered off after five minutes. On 15 minutes, the NG adopted attack

formation down the right, with target-woman Whoopi Goldberg popping out of a sub-space wormhole to head inches wide. Doctor 'Bones' McCoy was left complaining about his lack of covering fire from Sulu, and loads of other stuff. Meanwhile, at the other end, Will 'Captain's-Captain's-Number-One' Ryker was rarely troubled, except by throwaway love-interest sub-plots.

The first-half highlight was Doctor Beverley Crusher's turn-and-shot from six yards, which rattled the woodwork. Also rattled were the disappointing Spock and Data, who effectively cancelled each other out in their quest for logical midfield supremacy, trying to figure out how Dr Crusher apparently gets younger with each passing episode.

In the second half, the subtleties of plot and characterisation attempted by the NG were continually dashed by the slinky skills of Lieutenant Uhuru. Trails of Politically Correct crewmen were left goggling in her wake, doubtless pleased to see a mini-skirted minority at last breaking through at the highest level: space.

With the game deadlocked deep into extra time, the canny stopper Picard was caught out giving Mr Spock a dose of his own nerve-pinch as he strolled clear on goal looking for all the world like some green-blooded Martin Peters. The Trek captain, Kirk, proceeded to pull off the dead-ball play that has won the yellow/red/blues so many close contests in the past. He first confused the opposition with a lot of sub-Shakespearian mumbo-jumbo about the Power of Human Love, and then smartly smote home a trademark photon torpedo from the edge of the D. One-nil, sir!?! And just three seconds left on the clock!?!

As Kirk lifted the FU Cup, original Trek aficionadoes wiped the fake vaseliney sweat from their faces, squared their toupees and raised the roof with a beergut-busting rendition of the Final anthem.

All together now: 'And you'll ne-ver-Live-Long-And-Prosper . . . Alone . . . You'll never live . . .'

FAN-TASTIC FACT FILE

Grab a cuppa and a footy fact at the info superhighway's cyber-greasy spoon!?! Access the Treasury's Football Database – and find out *everything there is to know* about . . .

SHEFFIELD WEDNESDAY
Nickname: The Owls
Badge: Owl

OLDHAM ATHLETIC
Nickname: The Latics
Badge: Owl

LEEDS UNITED
Nickname: The Peacocks
Badge: Owl
Official club crest: Three owls and a dead sheep
Brand new badge: Psychedelic smiley
Brand new official club crest: 'I've Seen The Prodigy' poster

SIX OWLS and a dead sheep . . .

CHELSEA
Manager: Geoff Hurst
Secretary: Christine Matthews
Nickname: 'Butch' Wilkins
Fan slogan: Osgood Isgood
Funny-sounding goalies: Peter Bonetti; Peter Borota; Eddie Niedzwecki; Les Fridge
Big hair day: Ian Britton
Penultimate hair day: Clive Walker
Bad hair day: Tuesday

MIDDLESBROUGH
Honours: Anglo-Scottish Cup 1975–76
Manager: Malcolm Allison
Nickname: The Cleveland Cowboys
Local rivals: Berwick Rangers
Stoopid player names: Willie Woof, Peter Creamer, James Stewart
Famous baldie: David Armstrong
Cool deals: Bought Wilf Mannion, bloke with centre-parting, in first £1,000 transfer; sold useless David Mills for British record £500,000 to Ron Atkinson's WBA

CLYDE
Nickname: The Bully Wee
Kit: Don't know
Famous players: None
Weak Clyde-based pun for lease to headline writers: Bonnie and Clyde!?!
Local Rivals: Clydebank
Local rivals' famous player: Pat Nevin

CLYDE Not So Very Famous . . .

ARSENAL
Manager: Bertie Mee
Under-soil heating: Yes
Fantastic England players: Lee Dixon, Brian Marwood, Alan Smith, Paul Davis, Mickey Thomas, Roy 'Rocky' Rocastle, Nigel Winterbottom, Graham Rix
Fantastic famous fans: Arfur Mullard, Pete Murray, Bernie Winters, Schnorbitz
Famous manager: Herbert Chapman was a fat old bloke in black-and-white who murdered football in the 1930s. He invented the concept of the negative defensive formation, which left Chapman's Boring Arse with loads of trophies – and blood all over their hands . . .

BAD HAIR DAY at Disco Chelsea . . .

CLIVE WALKER

STEVE KEMBER

IAN BRITTON